The Surviving Past

Archaeological finds and excavations in Central Lancashire
by John Hallam

This book brings together in a condensed form the results of archaeological surveys and excavations carried out during the past ten years for the Central Lancashire Development Corporation.

Unlike most local history books its theme is not centred on a particular piece of research but was dictated by day to day contingencies of planning and development within the New Town's designated area. Consequently, it is a case book of historical detective stories bringing together for the first time material old and new.

It can be used as a guide book, not only to sites, but to the range of historical features that lie in many of the familiar, everyday things which surround us. For the interested reader or the research student it opens up new horizons of archaeological and historical possibilities not only within the New Town area of Central Lancashire but within the rest of the county and beyond.

D0185069

Published by Countryside Publications Limited, School Lane, Brinscall, Chorley, Lancashire.
Printed by Tamley-Reed Limited.
ISBN 0 86157 190 8

Contents

List of Illustrations

Foreword

by Sir Frank Pearson Bt MBE JP DL MA
Chairman of Central Lancashire Development Corporation

Central Lancashire Development Corporation is primarily concerned with new development to improve the prosperity of the area. However, the Corporation has from its inception, been conscious of the importance of safeguarding the archaeological heritage of Central Lancashire wherever possible.

The Outline Plan for Central Lancashire New Town, published by the Corporation in 1974, drew specific attention to this rich heritage and the need to provide for the preservation of older buildings and sites of archaeological interest. The investigation of sites prior to development was clearly of great importance in achieving this aim, and in 1975 the Corporation's Board retained John Hallam to act as the Corporation's Consultant Archaeologist.

The report which follows is a summary of the results of his work to date, which are encouraging and on which John Hallam is to be congratulated. Not only has his work with the Corporation resulted in this report which is a unique contribution to the historical knowledge of the area, but it has also involved identification, excavation and research on a number of significant sites.

This is a useful record of research within a relatively short period and it is my hope that the work begun here and recorded in this report can continue to make a significant contribution to the body of archaeological and historical knowledge which we have of our heritage.

Acknowledgments

Acknowledgments of help and grateful thanks for assistance in ways too numerous to mention are offered to:

The General Manager and officers and staff of the Central Lancashire Development Corporation.

The archivists and archaeologist of the Lancashire Record Office. The maps on pages 102, 103 appear with kind permission of the Lancashire Record Office.

The staff of the County Museum Service, the County Library (Local History Section) and the Harris Museum, Preston.

Members of the Chorley and District Historical and Archaeological Society, Leyland Historical Society and the West Lancashire Archaeological Society. These Societies not only shared their information and helped with advice and discussion, but took an active part in the excavations at Astley and made financial contributions also.

Individual mention must be made of the supervisors of the Job Creation Project of 1977: Linda Aiano, Norman Ball, Tim Gammon, Stanley Mycock, Jenny Russel and Edmund Southworth; and also as assistants to the Survey, Jennifer Lewis and Julie Hallam, and to George Bolton who helped with documentary research.

'The Surviving Past' was designed at Central Lancashire Development Corporation by Peter Coombs and Nick Cook; typesetting by Patricia Morgan.

Introduction

The archaeological surveys and excavations included in the following report were initiated by the Central Lancashire Development Corporation and were undertaken on their behalf by John Hallam, of the Central Lancashire Research Unit, Hesketh Bank, near Preston.

The aim of the Survey was to explore the archaeological and historical character of the New Town and to advise on sites and buildings revealed to be of importance.

Whilst not claiming to be comprehensive, the report shows the range of surviving archaeological and historical evidence. Combining archaeological research with historical studies, a more than expected historical heritage has been revealed.

Over 4000 years of continuous human settlement, ranging from Bronze Age tribesmen of the 19th century BC to cotton factory housewives of the 19th century AD, has been established.

A number of potential archaeological and historical sites and areas discovered in the course of the survey are discussed and attention has been drawn to those in danger of destruction.

Two excavations have been carried out, one at Astley Hall Farm, Chorley, and the other at Red Scar, Preston, in advance of the Astley Village and Roman Way developments.

The Astley excavation revealed the first Bronze Age ritual-burial site to be discovered in lowland Lancashire around the Ribble, and the second gave details of a suspected Roman road from Kirkham to Ribchester. The finds from Astley are on display in Astley Hall and a section of the Roman road has been preserved and will eventually be open to the public.

Field survey and documentary research has established the date and purpose of two lines of stone posts in Ambrye Meadows, Leyland. One of these field boundaries has been restored and presented as a local historical feature.

During the course of building surveys and demolition examples of early timber framing have been discovered. Some of these timbers have been recovered and can be used for reconstruction or as museum exhibits.

When the detailed survey reports are made available to the public, they will not only provide information concerning the various archaeological and historical discoveries, but should also point the way to a more informed understanding of the New Town's past, and perhaps, hopefully, towards more realistic policies of heritage conservation.

In presenting the following report it has been necessary for the purpose of clarity to include introductory outlines of some of the lesser known periods and to refer sometimes to discoveries and situations outside the New Town.

The opinions, errors and omissions are the responsibility of the author.

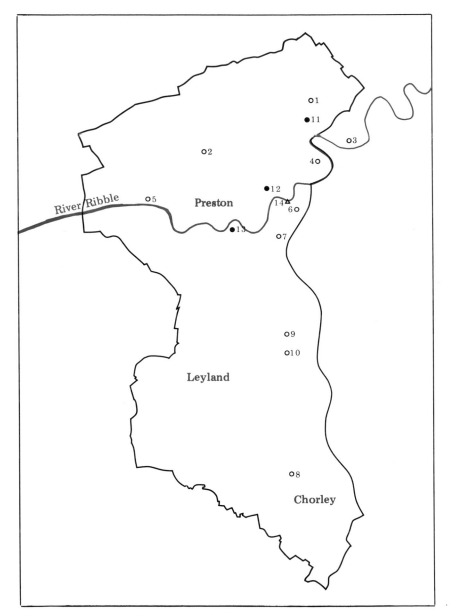

Prehistoric, Roman and
Viking sites within the
Central Lancashire New Town
boundary

Prehistory —
1 Grimsargh; perforated axe
    hammer
2 Sharoe Brook, Brookfield,
3 Elston Bottoms,
    Grimsargh; flat bronze axe
4 Higher Brockholes Farm,
    Ribble floodplain; barbed
    and tanged arrowhead
5 Preston Dock finds
6 Cuerdale; axehead and
    spearhead
7 Walton-le-Dale; axehead,
    spearhead, mirror handle
    and a harness mount
8 Astley Hall Farm, Chorley;
    Bronze Age Burial Site
9 Hawksclough; possible
    hilltop settlement site
10 Dovecote; possible hilltop
    settlement site

Roman —
11 Red Scar, Preston; Roman
    road
12 Fishwick, Preston;
    mortarium
13 The Flats, Winery Lane,
    Walton-le-Dale; Roman
    fort

Viking —
14 Cuerdale; Viking hoard

↑north

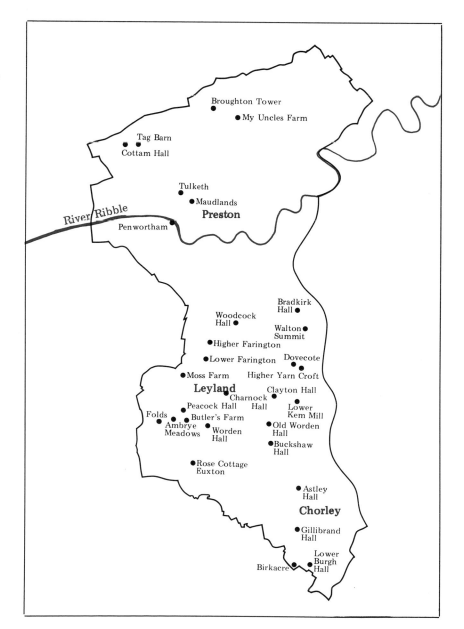

*Norman Conquest to
Industrial Revolution sites
within the Central Lancashire
New Town boundary*

↑ *north*

Broughton Tower

● My Uncles Farm

Tag Barn
Cottam Hall

Tulketh
● Maudlands

River Ribble

Preston

Penwortham

Bradkirk
Hall

Woodcock
Hall ●

Walton ●
Summit

● Higher Farington

● Lower Farington   Dovecote ●

Moss Farm ●   Higher Yarn Croft

Leyland   Clayton Hall

Charnock
Hall

Peacock Hall   ● Lower
Kem Mill

Folds ●   Butler's Farm ●

Ambrye   ● Old Worden
Meadows   ● Worden   Hall
    Hall

    ● Buckshaw
    Hall

● Rose Cottage
Euxton

● Astley
Hall

Chorley

● Gillibrand
Hall

    Lower
    Burgh
Birkacre ●   Hall

prehistory

Aboriginals
(Mesolithic, 10,000 — 3000 BC)

Although no direct evidence has been found within the New Town of the numerous hunting and food-gathering peoples who formed our aborigine population for a period of over 7000 years, it is potentially present.

Environment

At the beginning of the period the Lancashire coast and the Irish Sea did not exist as we know them today. The land, for example, between the coast and the Isle of Man was studded with lakes and scoured by rivers formed from the melt-waters of the shrinking glaciers. It was a land covered by sub-arctic trees and scrub and inhabited by wildfowl, small arctic mammals, reindeer and elk.

By the end of this early period the Irish Sea had formed and the Lancashire plain had become a low-lying coastal area, whilst the hinterland and the hills to the east were covered with mixed-oak forests, providing a habitat for wild pig, wild cattle and herds of red deer. All of these were hunted by man - their predator.

Early Post-Glacial

The first clue that man was present in Lancashire during this early post-glacial period came from an archaeological discovery near Blackpool over 10 years ago. The remains of an elk were discovered by a mechanical digger only 3 feet below the surface in a deposit of peaty-mud. This deposit had formed part of the edge of a post-glacial mere and a scientific investigation of the site showed that the elk had drowned during the winter and its body was trapped in the muds beneath the ice. The archaeological evidence revealed that the elk had been severely wounded by missiles and weapons of human hunters. Two barbed bone spear-points were discovered along with the skeleton, and a Carbon 14 date of about 10,000 BC was obtained from the deposit in which the skeleton was lying.

Camp Sites

The remains of aborigines' camp sites during the period from 8000 to 4000 BC have been found scattered extensively over the Lancashire and Yorkshire Pennines, which include the moors to the east of the New Town. Until recently it was thought that Lowland Lancashire was unoccupied during this period. However, as a result of archaeological research, two sites close to the New Town have been discovered. One of the sites was on former heathland in Mawdesley and the other is on the banks of the River Ribble, near Ribchester, and is still under investigation.

These camp sites are represented almost entirely by a scatter of flint tools and chipping debris, sometimes numbering thousands of pieces. Their distribution is widespread throughout Britain and Europe and are best preserved in sandy, well-drained soils or in fossilized horizons such as the podsol soils of the moors and heathlands.

The majority of the known camp sites in the north-west were discovered during the past hundred years by flint collectors who had little or no archaeological training; consequently much evidence has been lost. The number of these camp sites is not infinite. It is now essential that future discoveries should be archaeologically investigated so that the kind of success achieved at the elk site near Blackpool can be extended to the aborigine camp sites of this later period.

In 1981/82 some flint flakes and chippings were discovered during the excavation of the Roman site at Walton-le-Dale by the Department of the Environment's Archaeological Unit. They were close to the south bank of the river and represent the first Mesolithic site in the New Town.

Other areas within the New Town where watch should be kept for camp sites and finds of this period are the areas adjacent to former mosses and the low-lying swampy ground where peat and detritus muds occur. Also, areas where there are slight eminences formed of gravels and sandy or loamy soils, especially near the banks of rivers or streams. Such areas could have been former heathlands and are likely places where the tell-tale flints of a disturbed camp site might be discovered.

Early Settlers
(Neolithic, 3600 – 2000 BC)

Introduction

If the Mesolithic hunters and food-gatherers are regarded as the aborigines of our island, then the Neolithic communities can be seen to represent the first early settlers, who brought to our island new technologies and a new life style. It is now well established that these Neolithic immigrants came from the mainland of Europe where they had established such skills as flint mining; the quarrying of igneous rocks for the production of stone axeheads; weaving; pottery making and wood working. Agriculture replaced dependence on hunting and food-gathering, and more permanent settlements replaced the temporary hunting camps. However, there is evidence which indicates that the two cultures - Mesolithic and Neolithic - continued to live side by side for many generations. Neolithic communities were more highly organised than the Mesolithic folk, sharing a common stock of religious beliefs and social practices. The wealth of their culture is becoming more and more apparent as excavations and field work increases, revealing more of their wide ranging trading activities, and the astounding ability to erect large and complex structures of earth, stone and timber.

Finds and Sites

In Lancashire there is no evidence to date of developed Neolithic communities with large tribal centres and burial mounds. Whilst much needed aerial photography may reveal buried stone features which may remedy this deficiency, evidence for their presence still consists of the chance finds of stone and flint axe-blades and characteristic flint tools and missiles. Two sites in the county, one at Whalley and the other in Lancaster, both excavated for other archaeological purposes, revealed traces of Neolithic settlements in the form of pottery fragments, flint implements and chert-working. Palaeo-botanical evidence has revealed on the Lancashire plain the presence of forest clearance and regeneration dated to the Neolithic period.

Within the New Town a Cumbrian axe-blade and a leaf-shaped arrowhead have been found in Preston. Neolithic sites may occur in similar situations to those of the Mesolithic. General appeals ought to be made for finders to report discoveries of axe-blades so that find spots can be archaeologically examined for further evidence.

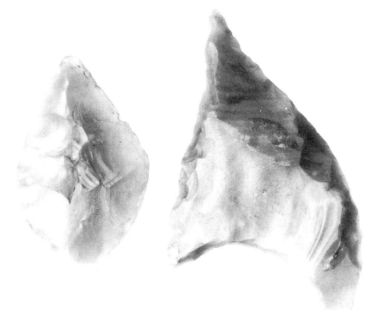

Arrowheads typical of the Neolithic period

Herders and Traders

(Early and Middle Bronze Age, 2000 — 800 BC)

Introduction

At the beginning of this period another influx of immigrants from the continent appeared in many parts of Britain and began to take over the local Neolithic communities. They are referred to as Beaker People. Their religious and social traditions differed markedly from those of the Neolithic, and there is some evidence to suggest that they may represent the first of the Celtic peoples to come into Britain. They are important, too, in so far that they introduced the first metals - bronze and gold - into this country.

Their presence in counties surrounding us has been established to a greater or lesser degree, but not in Lancashire itself. The reasons for this are not clear. However, communities which developed from an admixture of Neolithic and Beaker Peoples and known as Bronze Age Folk were certainly present in Lancashire, as their many ritual-burial sites testify. Other evidence in the form of flint implements, stone battle axes, perforated stone axe hammers, bronzes, pottery, whetstones, beads and minerals make this one of the richest periods of our local prehistory.

Palaeo-botanical evidence indicates that the prevailing climate for much of the period was warm and dry with winds blowing off the continent. Forest clearance continued with exposed soil subjected to dispersion by the eroding winds. The people themselves appear to have been semi-nomadic herdsmen, each group having its own tribal centre, which in some cases seem to mark the beginning of many of our Lancashire towns and villages.

It is probable that these tribes were led by chieftain families to whom trading, the exchanging of gifts and the accumulation of wealth were important. There also appears to have been a further class, probably a 'priestly' one, who were the custodians of accumulated knowledge, including mathematics and astrology.

The evidence for the Bronze Age in Lancashire consists of ritual-burial sites and chance finds of stone and bronze objects. When this evidence is studied it is apparent that the communities in Lancashire were in contact with those of other regions around the Irish Sea and elsewhere in Britain, sharing a common culture. However, regional and local variations and the absence of standardization are very noticeable; nowhere is this more apparent than in the case of ritual-burial sites and the burials and objects that are contained within them.

Ritual-Burial Sites

For the first time in Lancashire's prehistory we are presented with well-defined archaeological sites; numbering about 30 within the new county.

The term 'ritual-burial site' covers a variety of structures such as barrows, cairns, ring-cairns, stone circles, stake circles and ring banks. Whilst generally circular in shape these features can vary in size from a few feet in diameter to over a hundred. They were built of an admixture of materials such as earth, stones of all sizes, including large slabs sometimes moved from other areas, and wooden stakes and pillars. The presence and arrangement of both internal and external features, the number and positions of the burials, the manner of the burials and the contents of the cremation urns are in no two cases alike and cannot readily be summarized, although the following observations can be noted:

i) Burials do not occur in all these structures and when they do they are almost without exception cremations.

ii) Only a random selection of the deceased's bones were buried; some in urns, others directly in the ground. Pathological examination has shown that the remains represent men, women and children, and that in some cases more than one body is represented in the burial.

iii) It is obvious that these ritual-burial sites were not tribal cemeteries. What happened to the majority of the Bronze Age dead is not known.

iv) Grave goods such as bronze daggers and pins, in one case a piece of gold, flints, personal belongings made of bone, wood, amber and jet, and minerals such as quartz crystals, calcite and galena occur in some burials but not in others. When identifiable bronzes are present they are invariably of Early Bronze Age type. It appears that the custom of burying objects with the dead gradually faded out and had ceased during Middle Bronze Age times.

v)   The hand-made urns and accessory vessels are made of coarse pottery fired under bonfire conditions. They were usually decorated with geometric designs and in the case of the urns, on the collars and neck only. The designs were probably symbolic, but if so their meaning has, so far, eluded us.

The sites are widely distributed throughout the county. Many are to be found on ridges and high ground, others on the moorlands such as the Winter Hill area near Chorley, around Pendle Hill and on the Burnley Moors. Two recent discoveries have added significantly to the distribution pattern. They are both by streams; one in the village of Pendleton, near Clitheroe, the other on land behind Astley Hall, in Chorley.

The site at Astley Hall Farm is of special interest because it occurred on land owned by the Corporation and was excavated as part of the archaeological survey. (see page 33)

Bronze Implements

The majority of the bronze implements of the Early and Middle Bronze Age that are recorded have been discovered as chance finds and are either axe or spear heads. In the Early Bronze Age these implements were cast in open moulds made of stone; consequently they were flat and had to be hafted in a similar manner to the stone and flint ones. A fine specimen of these flat bronze axes was found just within the New Town at Elston Bottoms, Grimsargh, and is now in the Harris Museum, Preston. It is of a type found widespread in northern and western Britain and Ireland. Decorated specimens have been found at Pilling and at Read, above the Calder, near Whalley. Other bronzes have also been found along the Ribble and the Calder and at Bleasdale and Barrowford.

It has already been mentioned that a few small objects such as pins and dagger blades, made of bronze, have been discovered accompanying cremation burials. A bronze pin (now lost) is reported from the burial at Revidge, Blackburn, and a bronze dagger accompanied one of the burials at White Hall, Darwen. There is, of course, the possibility of a bronze object in Urn No 2 from Astley Hall Farm.

In the Middle Bronze Age, bi-valve moulds had been developed and new types of bronze axes (palstaves) and socketed spearheads were produced. Again, only a small number have been found in Lancashire. Their distribution differs from that of the Early Bronze Age specimens, the significance of which is not clear.

Those nearest to the New Town are two specimens from the peat-lands of Martin Mere, Rufford. A number of finds from the Pilling Mosses, supported by palaeo-botanical evidence, suggests that there were settlements in the moss-land areas. Once again, the peat areas, especially along the fringes, are important as archaeologically sensitive areas.

Flint and Stone Artefacts

Other artefacts, typical of the Early and Middle Bronze Age, are of flint and stone. Although bronze implements were available, flint and stone continued to be used and flint mined, especially in the early part of the period. Good quality flint enabled a high standard of flint craftsmanship to be achieved, producing beautifully made arrowheads, spearheads and polished axes. Some of these objects appear to be copies of bronze implements intended for ceremonial purposes only. The barbed and tanged arrowheads found in countless ritual-burial sites, are a well-known, characteristic implement of this prehistoric period.

Three barbed and tanged arrowheads have been found within the New Town, all in Preston. One comes from the Ribble flood-

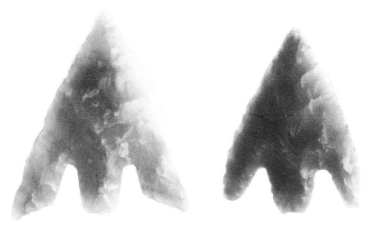

Barbed and tanged axe hammers typical of the Bronze Age

plain near Higher Brockholes Farm, a second above the Sharoe Brook on the Brookfield Estate, Ribbleton, and a third somewhere near Preston Dock.

Higher Brockholes and the land along the banks of Sharoe Green Brook and Eaves Brook (where Neolithic flint finds have also been made) are areas where possible settlement sites might occur. There is a Bronze Age ritual-burial site, for example, further upstream on the Ribble floodplain at Hacking Hall, between Ribchester and Whalley. Higher Brockholes appears to be a site of some antiquity and the finding of a Bronze Age arrowhead provides further evidence. Whilst chance finds of barbed and tanged arrowheads can be misleading, having been collector's pieces from time immemorial, there is no reason to doubt that two of the specimens are original finds, although the third one from the Preston Dock area is perhaps doubtful.

Perforated Stone Implements

Two types of stone implements appear during this period and likewise disappear towards the end of the early Bronze Age; they are battle axes and perforated axe hammers.

The battle axes have a wide distribution throughout Europe. Four specimens have been found in Lancashire but none occur in the New Town; the nearest ones are at Blackpool and Claughton. These battle axes are very elegantly made implements intended mainly for ceremonial purposes. Many are made from rock quarried on axe-factory sites, and when found within an archaeological context, are usually associated with inhumation burials. These artefacts could occur within the New Town and any find should be investigated immediately in case it represents a disturbed burial. Such a find could lead to an important site.

Perforated axe hammers are larger than battle axes and were obviously made for a different purpose, but what that purpose was is uncertain, hence the clumsy name. These implements are mostly chance finds and little is known of their archaeological context. Again, like many of the battle axes, some of them are made from rock associated with axe-factory sites, so that this connection, along with the methods of manufacture and their many similarities to the well-dated battle axes, places them undoubtedly in the Early Bronze Age period. The distribution of these axe hammers in Lancashire is predominantly in the lowland area.

Two have been found within the New Town, again in the Preston area. One, a rather damaged specimen now in the Harris Museum, is reported to have been found at a depth of four feet near the stone cross at Grimsargh. The second is half of a perforated stone implement described as an adze, which is rather unusual, and was found in the gravel of the Ribble floodplain at Preston, in 1892. It is possible that this find may have been a 'net sinker', belonging to a class of stone object that has received little archaeological study.

Other specimens may turn up at any time. If they do, the details of the circumstances of the find and the provenance need to be carefully checked. There is always the danger of false provenance resulting from secondary use by country folk.

Developing Tribal Communities
(Late Bronze Age and Iron Age, 1st millenium BC)

Introduction

The archaeological evidence for this period is more complex than that of the preceding period, especially towards its end when the native cultures were supplemented by richer cultures diversified by Roman conquests. In this period we have for the first time written records from Roman sources which provide us with details of life in Britain at that time.

In the past decade increased archaeological fieldwork, excavation and research have produced a mass of new evidence which has not yet been fully absorbed by archaeologists; consequently, new interpretations concerning this period are likely to emerge in the near future.

Bronze Artefacts

Bronzes are, again, the most important class of artefact for much of this period, especially in Lancashire. Introduction of lead into the bronze and improved casting techniques resulted in a vast increase both in production and range of types. In addition to axes, spears and rapiers, there are now swords and their fittings, shields, buckets, bowls, harness and cart fittings, and woodworking tools and many others.

The earliest recorded finds within the New Town come from Cuerdale and Walton-le-Dale (pages 28/29) and consist of two axe-heads and two spearheads of the late Bronze Age period, a mirror handle and a harness mount of the later Iron Age. The accounts of these finds since 1840 are somewhat confused and the identification of objects in the Harris Museum has been the subject of much discussion. However, it is certain that these finds were made and the find spot of those reported from Cuerdale is described in some detail. The axehead and spearhead, found at different times, were discovered on the flood plain about 380 yards from the Cuerdale Viking Hoard (see page 57). The other finds - a spearhead, axehead, the mirror handle and the harness mount - have no precise location.

Late Bronze Age metalwork,
Walton-le-Dale
Far left, socketed axe blade
Left, harness fitting
Right, socketed spearhead

During the excavation of Preston Docks (1885) a bronze
spearhead was found at the base of the gravel along with other
finds to be described below.

Bronze hoards, some of them very large, are a feature of this
period. Many of them appear to have been deliberately hidden by
bronze smiths or wealthy owners whilst others may represent
votive offerings thrown in a cave or marsh. Two important ones
have been discovered in Lancashire: one from Pilling Moss
(Warrington Museum) and the other from the Iron Age Hillfort at
Whalley. This hoard, which is now in the British Museum, was
remarkable in having two rare gold ornaments included in it. No
established hoards have been found in the New Town, but it is
just possible that the objects found at Walton-le-Dale and Cuerdale
may have been small hoards.

The Preston Dock Finds

When the Preston Docks were being constructed around 1885, a number of remarkable finds were made which are unique in the north-west. Apart from the bronze spearhead already mentioned, there were two dug-out canoes, the skulls of about 24 human beings, skulls and antlers of the large red deer, numbering about 100 individuals, 43 skulls with horns of wild cattle and the remains of a few horses. These were found between 13 and 15 feet below the surface which was around three feet above Ordnance Datum. In addition, between 8 and 15 feet down, wooden piles were discovered with roughly pointed ends driven into the gravel associated with some two or three feet of brushwood. Whilst caution must be exercised in using these finds as archaeological evidence, the possibility cannot be ruled out that some, if not all, are chronologically related and may well represent some kind of settlement.

Other Finds

Other objects characteristic of this period and found in other parts of the north-west, but not so far in the New Town, include stone beehive-type rotary querns and carved stone heads. Some of the latter representing Celtic gods, may well belong to the Iron Age, such as the one in the Harris Museum found near the River Ribble.

Pottery in some parts of Britain was mass produced and traded, but in the north it is poorly represented. When it does occur, usually during archaeological excavations, it is coarse, thick and gritty and not always easy to identify, even by experts. Loom weights and sling stones made from either baked clay or stone sometimes occur as chance finds.

Wooden objects, other than dug-out canoes, can survive in waterlogged conditions. These should be looked for near suspected sites; for example, the Ribble flood plain at Cuerdale. Mechanical gravel-diggers have recovered dug-out canoes, or

A timber from Kate's Pad, Pilling

fragments of them, but anything smaller would be destroyed or overlooked. A Late Bronze Age trackway, made of 'sleepers' placed end to end, has been discovered in the Pilling area where it is known as Kate's Pad. No others have been reported from the Lancashire mosses although they might well have occurred but not recognised as having any archaeological significance.

Hillforts and Settlements

The term 'hillfort' covers a wide variety of defended sites, not all necessarily situated on the tops of high hills.

No hillforts or defended sites of this later prehistoric period within the first millennium BC have been recognised within the New Town area. There is, of course, always the possibility that the site of Penwortham Castle could have been a defended site in prehistoric times. Other areas of high ground in Tulketh, Walton-le-Dale and Cuerden are further possibilities where buried ditches and traces of slighted or eroded ramparts might occur.

In a recent survey of the Cuerden Valley Park, two possible hilltop defended settlement sites have been located at Hawksclough and Dovecote, on the east side of the River Lostock. They have some features in common with the hillfort at Portfield, near Whalley.

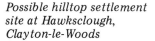

Possible hilltop settlement site at Hawksclough, Clayton-le-Woods

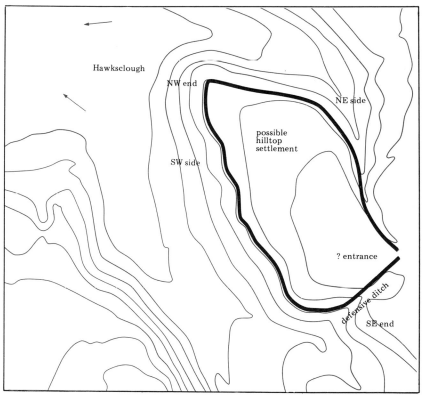

Farming complexes similar to those revealed by aerial photography in Northumberland, and elsewhere, composed of enclosures with circular huts, cattle corrals and small adjoining fields, may be present in our area, but they have yet to be found.

Conclusions

When all the archaeological evidence within the New Town for this period is considered together with Roman and later place name evidence, the outcome strongly suggests that in the Preston area there might well have been a tribal centre similar to those more strongly indicated in other parts of Lancashire, such as Pilling, Warton, Whalley and Colne.

It is unfortunate that we do not know exactly where the mirror handle and the harness mount from Walton-le-Dale were found. They were both prestige articles and suggest the possibility of a chieftain's settlement. It may not be a coincidence that there is every appearance of there being an important, non-military Roman establishment also situated in Walton-le-Dale.

It is perhaps not surprising that the Preston area shows a strong possibility of being important during the Iron Age, and the likely place of a tribal centre.

The Bronze Age site at Chorley indicates early settlement, which no doubt continued throughout the later prehistoric period. Local place names of early Celtic derivation tend to support this possibility. The Astley Hall Farm site cannot be the only one to have survived, there must be others in the area. Finds may have been made but never reported. In the meantime, if patient search is made, some day, perhaps with the help of aerial photography, the necessary clues may be found.

Bronze Age Burial Site
(Astley Hall Farm, Chorley)

Discovery

The chance discovery of this archaeological site at Astley Hall Farm, Chorley in 1963 was typical of many archaeological discoveries. In this case it was made by an observant farmer who, when carrying out digging work with his tractor, discovered that he had disturbed a prehistoric burial urn. When the farm was acquired by the New Town for Astley Village development in 1974, the site of the original discovery became available for further investigations.

Obviously no surface features of the prehistoric site had survived, so that the recovery of further evidence depended upon sub-soil features lying in the sandy soil. The search for these

Bronze Age Burial Site, Astley Hall Farm, Chorley View of excavations, 1976

features was made more difficult by the presence of farm building foundations and buried farm debris.

Excavations 1974 - 77

Excavations were carried out between 1974 and 1977, when, in addition to the original discovery, a further urn burial was located and four other cremations buried in shallow pits. Part of the site had been destroyed by tractor digging so that this number of burials may not have been the complete total. Four of the six burials occurred within a central area enclosed by a circular ditch or trench, some 36 feet in diameter; the remaining two, both in pits, were found on the edge of this circular feature at the southern end.

Although there had been much disturbance, the southern end of the circle did not appear to be complete, but terminated as if to form an entrance. Also in this area, just outside the circle, the remains of what appeared to have been a cobbled area were encountered, probably the remains of a forecourt. Thirty feet away from the entrance, also in a southerly direction, was a pit containing about 30 sherds of prehistoric pottery, not of the collared urn type, and a few flints. There was also charcoal and signs of burning. So far no further examples of pottery of this kind have been located in the north-west and possible parallels elsewhere are uncertain. The significance of this pit in relation to the ritual-burial site is at present uncertain.

Three further pits, but containing no remains, were also discovered; one in the central area close to the burials and the other two outside the circle to the east (see page 35). It is possible that these pits carried timbers and that the circular trench represented the remains of a timber circle. If so, it could have been similar in some respects to the smaller of the two well-known circles at Bleasdale, near Garstang.

A large area around the circle to the south was excavated when the remaining farm buildings were demolished in 1976; but no further features of the prehistoric period were discovered.

Plan of site

Key

U	*burial urn*
C	*cremation*
f	*flint*
rp	*rubbish pit*

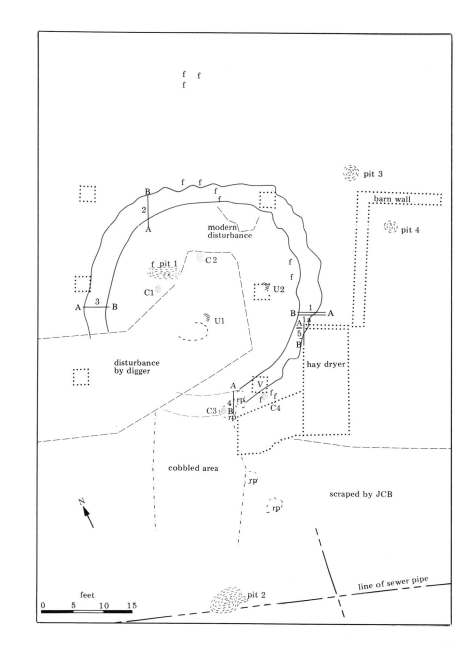

The Burials

The burials themselves contained several interesting features. When the first urn was found in 1963 not all of it was recovered, it having broken and collapsed before removal. In the initial stage of the excavations the site of this urn was rediscovered and some of the missing pieces and contents were recovered. These included two objects: one a small flint knife of a type commonly associated with burials, which, like the bones, had been burnt. The other object was a beautifully struck flake of igneous rock of the type used in Neolithic times for the manufacture of stone axeblades. This specimen could well have come from the Lake District, it had not been burnt and was an unusual find in many respects. It seems to suggest that the Astley Hall Farm site dates to the early stages of the Early Bronze Age when axe factory sites were still in production in the Lake District and that there may have been some connection between the two places.

The second urn discovered during the course of the excavations (page 37) contained, in addition to cremated human bones, charcoal, earth and pebbles, fragments of a miniature collared urn and fragments of a small wooden object, probably a tiny bowl or cup. One large piece of cremated bone, part of a left femur, bore a well defined green stain at the time of discovery. It appears to have been caused by the breakdown of copper or bronze and may well be all that remains of a bronze pin, not an unusual find in this context.

Cremated Remains

Pathological examination of the cremated remains revealed the following:

Urn 1 — the remains of an adult, probably over 40 years of age, may have been a female. There were signs of osteo-arthritis. A second younger body may also have been present.

Collared urn no.2, Astley Hall Farm, Chorley, discovered 1963

Urn 2 — the remains of a juvenile of about 7 years of age. Remains included the stained bone mentioned above.

Cremation 1 — probably only one body but differences in bone size make it probable that more than one body was included.

Cremation 2 — the remains are likely to be those of a child or adolescent.

Cremation 3 — there only appears to be the remains of one body and there is evidence of what appears to be the deliberate breaking of the bones after cremation.

Cremation 4 — the remains of an adult. Here there is the possibility of the intentional selection of bones and, again, evidence of deliberate breaking.

Flint and Stone Finds

The only other class of objects to be discovered on the site which remains to be discussed is that of flint, chert and stone. The flint and chert specimens totalled 39 pieces. Of these, 11 were associated with the six burials, some of them burnt, whilst a further four were found in the pit beyond the entrance. Thirteen pieces were found around the circular ditch or trench and a further 11 pieces were picked up away from the site, at distances varying from 15 feet to over a hundred. Of the total 39 pieces, nine were tools, three were utilized pieces, and the remaining 27 represent chipping waste. The tools included one plano-convex knife, 4 scrapers, a notched implement and three others - the precise use of which is not known. All the identifiable pieces were small and rather scrappy and appear, as is often the case in this area, to have been made from locally available materials recovered from streams and river gravels.

The stone object discovered near the edge of the circle was a small pebble of quartzitic sandstone, pecked out to form what appears to be the tip of a phallus. However, no other objects of this type are known in the north-west, but better defined specimens have been recovered from the flint mines of south-east England. There, they were carved from chalk and were associated with the production of flint axe-blades. Is this phallus tip from Astley Hall Farm another link between the ritual-burial site there and the axe-blade industry? The other possible link, the igneous flake associated with Urn 1, has already been described.

Similar specimens to the phallus under discussion could have occurred on other ritual-burial sites in the county but may not have been recognised during earlier excavations. There is a case for arguing that phalli could have formed part of the rituals carried out on these ritual-burial sites, and that if they were made locally from available materials then the Astley find is the type of object that would have been produced.

Conclusions

The excavations at Astley Hall Farm have, from one chance find, resulted in establishing the presence of an Early Bronze Age ritual-burial site; hitherto unsuspected in this area. This discovery has not only enriched local history, marking the beginnings of human settlement in Chorley, but has made a significant contribution to the prehistory of Lancashire.

From another point of view it also represents the first archaeological discovery to be made within the New Town development during the course of the Archaeological Survey.

ROMAN

43 – 406 AD

Introduction

The Roman occupation has been the well established beginning to the documentary history of Britain since the 17th century. However, since the Victorian period and particularly in recent years a growing volume of archaeological discoveries of all kinds has extended our knowledge of Roman Britain far beyond the limitations of the documentary evidence. The once shadowy 'Ancient Britons', for example, that the Roman army warred against and conquered have now emerged as a mixture of Celtic peoples with a rich culture supported by slavery and commercial activities. Inter-tribal warfare and raiding were widespread, aggravated by invasions from Europe of Celtic communities displaced by Caesar's invasions of Gaul. It was, however, the rich corn growing areas of southern and central England that were mainly affected by these changes. In the more pastoral north, change was more gradual. Here, the Roman armies brought wealth and new opportunities, but even after 400 years of occupation the Romans do not seem to have fundamentally changed the basic way of life. Movements of people undoubtedly took place, but it was left to Christianity and the Saxon and Viking invasions to absorb and overshadow the Celtic peoples and their culture in the north-west. Even so, the basic economy of pastoralism and subsistence farming continued.

The Roman occupation of Lancashire was primarily a military one. It established a number of forts such as Kirkham, Ribchester and Lancaster and designed a road system which served to police the area as well as being a part of the general British network. Around the forts, excavational evidence has revealed the presence of civil settlements or military towns in which the soldiers, locals and foreign peoples mixed and inter-married.

The details of the military changes throughout the period of the occupation and the growth of the adjacent settlements are in the process of being worked out as opportunities for excavation and research occur. Archaeological work in the past has, naturally, concentrated on the known Roman fort sites which in Lancashire were established around 79 AD, the year of Agricola's campaign. They remained in use sporadically till the end of the 4th century when they were abandoned. Civilian occupation continued and then, it too, gradually disappeared.

The main Roman evidence within the New Town is the site of The Flats, Walton-le-Dale and two main roads running north to south and east to west - Wigan to Lancaster and Kirkham to Ribchester, crossing in Preston at Fulwood.

Sites and Finds

Walton-le-Dale

The site at Walton-le-Dale occupies an area known as The
Flats, which is situated on the floodplain between the Ribble,
where it swings round at Walton Bridge, and the confluence of the
River Darwen, further downstream.

The site was discovered by Hardwick in 1852 who was
monitoring workmen extracting gravel from a mound which was
thought to contain the remains of some Cromwellian battle.
Instead, a series of undoubtedly Roman objects were found.
Subsequent excavations in the area revealed mortared stone floors,
a wall and gravelled surfaces. The objects eventually found their
way into the Harris Museum and Hardwick published his
discoveries in his History of Preston.

Between 1947 and 1960, Ernest Pickering, with the help of
the Walton-le-Dale Archaeological Society, carried out a series of
small scale trenching excavations. The presence of Roman type
buildings was established on two main sites. One (Site 1) was
situated between the northern loop of the former ox-bow of the
Darwen (now filled in) and the Ribble itself; the other (Site 2)
within the loop of the ox-bow. The western part of the site was
truncated by a dug channel short-circuiting the ox-bow. This river
diversion seems to have been carried out sometime between 1758
and 1845.

These excavations revealed that the buildings, dated to
around 100 AD were destroyed by fire about 120 AD, and then
replaced with more substantial buildings. These appear to have
been demolished about the middle of the 2nd century. Several
buildings were involved but details are wanting. The excavations
were limited to narrow trenches by the restraints of market
gardening activities. Under such circumstances the interpretation
of features can be arbitrary and sometimes misleading. However,
the excavations undoubtedly established that there is a Roman
site present capable of producing worthwhile evidence.

A further consideration which heightens the importance of
this site is that it does not appear to be a typical Roman fort.
Pickering sees in it the work of the Roman military and the site as

a fortified port. Nothing specifically military has come to light in any of the excavations or finds, and further, it is too close to either Kirkham or Ribchester to fit into the usual Roman pattern of spacing forts. It is quite possible that it was an important civilian site of some sort which had access to the sea. It was certainly well placed to be the latter, occupying as it did a very defensible stretch of tidal river.

Evidence which could support the possibility of Walton-le-Dale being an important civilian settlement came to light unexpectedly during the survey when unrecorded finds from this site were being examined in the Harris Museum. It consisted of two sherds of decorated pottery of an unusual type (pages 44 and 45). Whilst their association with Walton-le-Dale is not proven, there is no reason, after careful consideration, to doubt it; and their 2nd century date fits perfectly with the known chronology of the site.

The two sherds have been identified as a fragment of a decorated bowl and a fragment of a lamp handle. They appear to be of Cnidian ware, a high quality fabric superior to the well-known Samian ware. It originated in the eastern Mediterranean and only a few examples are known in Europe; it is very rare in Britain.

Excavations 1981 - 83 (see pages 44 and 45)

In 1981/82 and 1983, excavations on this site were carried out by the Department of the Environment's Archaeological Unit for Lancashire and Cumbria, directed by Adrian Olivier.

About two-thirds of an acre was investigated and the evidence suggests some kind of military establishment perhaps used for storage and supply. The features revealed were a section of road lying roughly on a north-south axis with two side streets on the north side; regular lines of post holes between these side streets showing that long, rectangular buildings had stood there; and areas of burnt clay, highly fired, which seemed to represent furnaces or kilns, but no indication of their purpose.

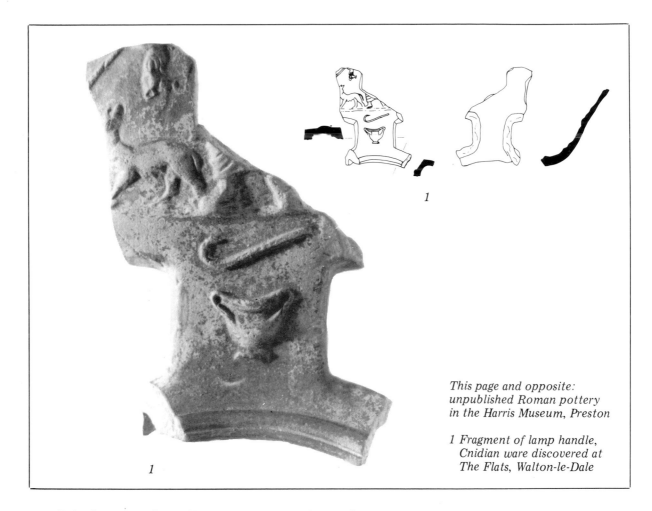

This page and opposite:
unpublished Roman pottery
in the Harris Museum, Preston

1 Fragment of lamp handle,
Cnidian ware discovered at
The Flats, Walton-le-Dale

It is clear that these discoveries are not those of a conventional Roman fort. The possibilities are that the site could have covered up to fourteen acres and was an important part of the Roman military network in the north-west. However, the full details of the excavation will not be clear until the post-excavational work and analyses of samples has been completed.

Excavations are to continue.

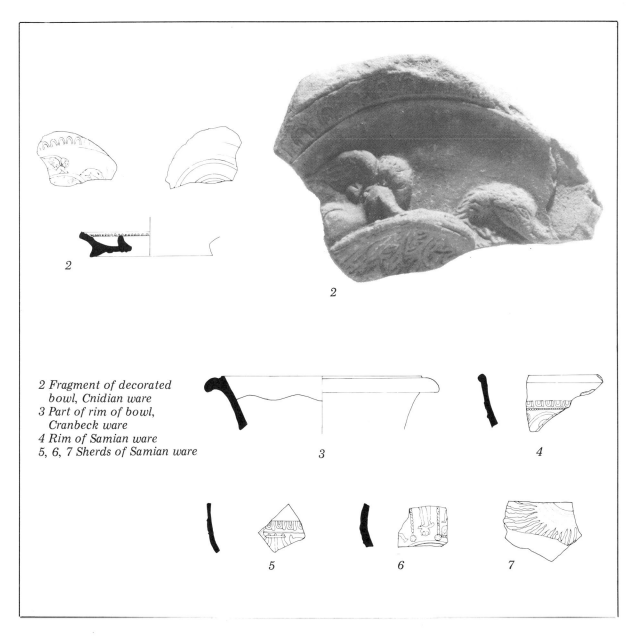

2

2

2 Fragment of decorated
   bowl, Cnidian ware
3 Part of rim of bowl,
   Cranbeck ware
4 Rim of Samian ware
5, 6, 7 Sherds of Samian ware

3

4

5

6

7

Fishwick, Preston

Another unexpected Roman find on display in the Harris Museum, the significance of which has gone unnoticed during the 50 years since its discovery, is an intact, late 3rd century mortarium (below). It was found in a sandpit in Fishwick on the

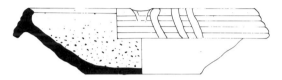

opposite side of New Hall Lane from Preston Cemetery (information from B J N Edwards). Mortaria were generally used for the pounding and preparing of food. The intactness of the Fishwick one suggests that it may have come from a disturbed grave where it would have been included as an accompanying utensil. As Roman law forbade burials within towns, graves have often been found alongside roads outside towns. If this mortarium represents a grave then there could be a Roman road or settlement nearby. Is there a connection here with Walton-le-Dale? Fishwick would be on line with a direct route to Ribchester and it is fairly close to Walton-le-Dale.

This sandpit would repay further investigation.

Coins and Other Chance Finds

Most of the coin finds, either in hoards or as single finds, were made during the last century, although a few have been recorded since. In most cases the exact find spot is not known, so that the finds are of limited archaeological value. Roman coins continue to be found but such is the state of the coin collecting market and metal detecting activities that few are being recorded and seldom does an archaeologist have opportunity to examine the find spot.

The burying of hoards in the first place was a random event but the possibility always exists that a road or settlement was not far away. As with the Late Bronze Age metal hoards we do not know who buried them or whether they represent savings or loot. Dateable coins found within the New Town range throughout the entire period of the Roman occupation.

One hoard is worthy of special note: the one from Chorley, found in a pot in 1820. The find, consisting of nine bronze and silver coins and silver jewellery, is in the British Museum. Dated by the coins about 140 AD, the silver jewellery consists of a pair of fine silver brooches or fibula and a fine silver chain to which they were presumably attached. Finds such as this are rare in the north-west. The brooches are of native design, being of a type which was developed in the north during the first half of the 2nd century. They were sometimes decorated with red enamel and represent native Celtic craftsmanship stimulated by Roman and continental influence and responding to the increased wealth brought in by the Roman occupation. This find has been inadequately published and its existence is known only to a few.

Roman Roads

Roman roads have excited considerable interest and study. They can be well defined features on the landscape and are often a focal point for local antiquarian interest, both informed and uninformed. They also present a comparatively straightforward type of fieldwork which can be pursued by those with only limited time for their archaeological activities. The pursuit of Roman roads is as old as antiquarianism itself, consequently discussion on their possible direction and whereabouts is widespread throughout society journals and Victorian local histories.

How long the roads remained in use after the Roman period and how far they determined later settlement is another subject which has received much discussion. In some areas the roads appear to have remained in use during the Dark Ages, in other areas they soon went out of use. Much would depend upon whether skilled maintenance was required to keep the roads open, especially where they were dependent upon bridges and grading. Road maintenance then, as today, depended upon a central authority to provide the skill and cover the cost. It is unlikely that any such authority existed in post-Roman Britain. The Roman roads were built primarily for carrying Roman regiments, cavalry and wheeled vehicles for supply. The traditional trackways and bridlepaths, not requiring maintenance, were no doubt more serviceable to the local communities.

Roman Roads in the New Town

Two Roman roads cross the New Town: one running north to south connecting the presumed site at Wigan with the fort at Lancaster, and the other running east to west, connecting the forts of Kirkham and Ribchester. They cross at Fulwood in Preston.

The North-South Road

The best starting place for tracing this road is at Fisher's

Farm in Charnock Richard (NGR 560160) on the 250 ft contour. From here the projected line runs northwards and takes in a stretch of Pear Tree Lane before crossing Euxton Lane and passing close to Buckshaw Hall and Old Worden Hall - where a Roman coin hoard was found in the last century. The land between Euxton Lane and Dawson Lane to the north is now occupied by the Ministry of Defence and cannot be entered. However, immediately on the north side of Dawson Lane, behind Leyland Golf Club is Gravel Hole Wood (NGR 564214), another eminence similar to that at Fisher's Farm. It could have been used as a sighting point by the Roman surveyors.

In 1977, during the course of the survey, the land behind Lancaster Lane, Clayton-le-Woods, being developed for housing, was examined whilst construction work was in progress. On the projected line of the Roman road traces of worked sandstone slabs were observed in the spoil from drainage trenches. Sandstone blocks had been observed in a section near Pear Tree Lane in the 19th century and on another site in Coppull excavated by the Chorley Archaeological Society.

Northwards there are two further traces of the road on the projected line. One is a stretch of land boundary and right of way in Cinder Path Wood by Cuerden Hall, and the other is a stretch of road now known as Meanygate in Bamber Bridge. When Hardwick noted this feature in 1855 it was known as Mainway Gate. After this the road presumably alters alignment, that is if it is the same road as the one observed crossing The Flats by the Roman site in Walton-le-Dale. The Ribble was fordable immediately downstream from Walton Bridge. Historical references give hints of the route taken through Preston where it crossed Preston Moor and joined the Kirkham to Ribchester road, according to Hardwick, between the Withy Trees and the Barracks.

It does seem, when all the evidence is considered, that a good case exists for the projected line of this Roman road. More fieldwork needs to be carried out aided by the study of suitable aerial photographs. In addition, every opportunity should be taken to examine any available land on this line. This method proved successful on the east to west road at Red Scar.

Could it be more than a coincidence that this road passes very close to the halls of Buckshaw, Old Worden, Clayton and Cuerden?

The East - West Road

The line of this road appears on the 1845 Ordnance Survey six inch map, based on aggers observed by antiquarians and surveyors. The memory of part of this road is enshrined in the modern name 'Watling Street Road'.

Roman road at Red Scar, Preston
Excavations showing ditches and remains of gravel surface

In 1976, during the course of the survey, a linear feature on the line of the road was observed on two aerial photographs, crossing land included in a development programme at Red Scar. The two photographs each showed a different half of the feature which was divided by the old crematorium road. They were scarcely visible on the ground.

It was decided, as part of the 1977 Job Creation Project, to excavate this feature. Whilst it seemed more than likely that it was part of the Roman road, confirmation was desirable and so, too, were details of repair and length of time in use; evidence which is sadly lacking for our area.

The Excavation of the Roman Road, Red Scar

The excavation took place in the summer of 1977 and consisted of two trenches sectioning the road. The first one, trench number 1, was close to the hedge where the road runs just north of a pond by the old crematorium road, and the second, trench number 2, was across the end of the feature on the western edge of the field. The positioning of trench number 1 was chosen on the grounds that the road was reasonably well defined at this point and that if it did prove to be Roman and worthy of presentation it could be included with the fishing pond as a small landscape feature.

Trench number 1 determined that the distance apart of the two boundary ditches was 78 feet. Boundary ditches are not always features of Roman roads, and these at Red Scar no doubt formed part of the initial survey and clearing phase. Later, they would indicate the area to be kept cleared for maintenance and security purposes.

Between these two boundaries the road consisted of a loosely gravelled surface flanked by two drainage ditches about 29 feet apart. The section revealed that the sub-soil upon which the road rested was composed of reddish clay. In the first phase of the road's use the surface had been cleared of vegetation and weathering of the reddish clay, thickest in the centre, indicated a period of use. Attempts to repair this earthen surface were indicated by the inclusion of occasional pebbles. A dark humus horizon above this weathered surface suggests that the road went out of use for a while or carried only occasional light traffic. The presence of a thin band of charcoal, representing the burning-off of light vegetation, marks the beginning of the next phase of use.

A layer of fine red sand and light gravel was laid next as a foundation for the road surface. In the centre for a distance of about 7 feet the foundation was banked up to provide the camber. The surmounting hard core, composed of large and small pebbles, was compacted but in no way fixed with any binding material.

Excavations in progress at Red Scar

Down the centre of the road there was indication of a line of larger stones, but there was no sign of curb stones along the edges to contain the gravel surface. Here and there the road surface showed signs of patching with larger pebbles.

As the road surface was only some 6 inches below the top of the plough soil, no evidence of further details of the history of the road presented themselves. After the road fell into disuse a grass-type vegetation colonised the surface, a top-soil developed and the presence of the road was obscured. There are no signs that it formed a feature of later settlement in the area.

A sherd of Roman pottery was recovered from the top of one of the ditches. It had formed part of the rim of a shallow basin and was made of a fine, light grey fabric, dated to the 3rd century AD. No further sherds were found and the significance of this one - apart from confirming the Roman status of the road and its use during the 3rd century - is not clear.

The second trench, trench number 2, revealed similar features to those already described and it confirmed the alignment of the road.

Whilst work was being carried out towards the presentation of the excavated road as an ancient monument, two further finds were made: the pinch-decorated base of a small vase or ointment jar, and a glass paste melon bead. The latter is of interest because melon bead necklaces were favoured by the Samatian Cavalry, some of which were stationed at Ribchester.

Whilst these three finds may represent losses by travellers on the road, they may also represent evidence of a settlement nearby.

The area would repay further fieldwork, aerial photography and documentary research.

ANGLO-SAXON AND VIKING

406-1066 AD

Introduction

Within these 650 years, two further invasions or major folk movements took place in Britain - the Anglo-Saxon and Viking; the coming of Christianity can perhaps be reckoned as a third, rather different type of invasion.

Compared to the Roman period the archaeological evidence for the Dark Ages is slight. However, increased archaeological evidence during the past twenty years involving the all-period approach to sites, revealed by aerial photographs, is at last throwing light upon this darkness. Unfortunately, there have been no developments of this kind in Lancashire, the main evidence for settlement still depending upon place name studies.

The finds throughout the county are small in number and consist of a few isolated graves, stone crosses, coin hoards and metal objects. Descriptions of Victorian discoveries referring to this period are not always easy to interpret when the finds have been lost or site details are lacking.

Chance finds of a few graves have occurred in lowland Lancashire; the closest to the New Town being at Claughton, Inskip and Blackrod. They sometimes occur in the remains of a ploughed-out barrow and can be identified by grave goods such as personal ornaments and swords and iron weapons.

Cuerdale Hoard
Coins of St Edmund to
commemorate his death,
869 AD

Cuerdale Hoard

The single Dark Age find within the New Town is a major one and of European significance. It consisted of a Viking treasure chest which was discovered on the banks of the Ribble near Cuerdale Hall in 1840. The chest of wood, lined with lead, contained over 7000 coins, silver ornaments, silver ingots, hack silver and four bone pins and a needle.

The coins include specimens from known Anglo-Saxon mints, a large number from an unknown Viking one and others from Europe and the Orient. They date the deposition of the hoard to about 900 AD.

The hoard has been split up and distributed to several museums and a few private collections; the bulk of the hoard being in the British Museum. Locally, there is a representative collection in the Merseyside Museum, a small collection in the Harris Museum, Preston, and a further collection in private possession.

The coins were studied in great detail at the time of discovery but the remainder of the hoard has received less attention. There is no up-to-date detailed description of the hoard available for study, although research is in progress.

The contents of the Cuerdale chest could represent accumulated trading wealth of a local Danish or Scandinavian trader which was hidden during this time of trouble. Piracy and

Coins of St Alfred (Cuerdale Hoard, Harris Museum)

raiding in the Irish Sea and along the coast of Lancashire may have threatened Danish trading which invoked the military action of Cnutr. Settlements at the mouth of the Ribble, which was no doubt on an important trade route, would be particularly vulnerable. One final point in this respect is that there was an oral tradition in Walton-le-Dale, recorded in 1810, to the effect that 'by standing on the bridge at Walton and looking towards Ribchester one could gaze over the richest treasure in England'. There seems no reason to doubt the authenticity of this tradition. The fact that the prophecy should be finally vindicated is as remarkable as the discovery of the treasure itself. A reasonable explanation of the tradition is that some event must have impressed itself upon the community for it to become enshrined in local folklore. Secondly, it argues for continuity of settlement, enabling the tradition to be passed on from one generation to another.

This remarkable discovery is very little known in Lancashire and at no time had it been possible for the public to see it or even a part of it on display, until the Viking Exhibition at the British Museum in 1980.

However, what concerns us here is the significance of the discovery in terms of local archaeology. From the time of discovery to the present day there has been speculation on how the hoard came to be there. Known historical events have been studied in the hope that they might provide a clue.

During the 10th century in both York and Dublin, there were vigorous trading settlements, whilst others around the coasts of the Irish Sea appear to have been centred on the Isle of Man. The Danes were in York, the Norwegians in Dublin and the Irish Sea area. A flourishing trade was established but not political unity, which resulted from time to time in raiding and warfare between one group and another. There is evidence that the Danes raided Dublin under the leadership of Cnutr in 903 AD - the date often claimed for the deposition of the hoard. The Danes were defeated and some believe they hid their pay chest or war chest at Cuerdale.

Settlements and Place Name Evidence

Place name evidence suggests that throughout the Dark Ages there were settlements within the New Town area occupied initially by groups of indigenous Celtic peoples, later to be supplemented by Saxon and Viking groups.

Whilst Preston's religious traditions may date no further back than the Norman Conquest, the place name evidence and geographical position of Eccleston to the south indicate the presence there of an early Christian settlement.

In the latter part of the period the possibility of Viking settlements along the Ribble in the Preston area and on the higher ground to the south has to be considered.

Later evidence of settlement names and field names included in monastic and estate records and mediaeval legal documents, both etymologically and geographically point to Norse settlement south of the Ribble around Cuerden, Brinscall and the eastern part of the township of Leyland as well as north of the Ribble around Grimsargh, Goosnargh and Haighton. 'Grimsargh', 'Goosnargh', 'Anglezarke', 'Gunolfsmoor', 'Ugthred', 'Brinscall', 'Scalecroft' are some of the more obvious clues.

These considerations of Dark Age settlement reinforce what has already been stated regarding continued archaeological work and surveillance in these riverine areas, and that every development or soil disturbance should be explored and monitored wherever and whenever possible. This cannot be too strongly emphasised.

Norman Conquest -
Industrial Revolution

1066 - 1760 AD

Introduction

Whilst the period from 1066 to the end of the 18th century was one of many changes, it shares much with the previous periods and can be seen as a further phase in human change and development. For example, animal and human muscle power, aided by wind and water were still the main sources of motive power. For much of the period, timber and peat provided heat for warmth and craft manufacture. Timber, clay, brick and stone were the basic building materials, and as in earlier times man could travel no faster than the fastest horse. Two things distinguish the 2nd millennium AD from the previous millennia: firstly, that we are living at the end of it, and, secondly, that there is, understandably, considerably more surviving archaeological and historical material than from previous periods. Not least in importance is the vast collection of documentary material which increases in volume as we approach nearer our own time.

Whilst the research into documents is the proper task of the historian, there are documents, including maps, which have direct bearing on land use, buildings and economic activities which are the concern of archaeology. There is a vast number of these documents in the Lancashire Record Office alone, many of which such as manorial court rolls, have yet to be transcribed and published.

Mediaeval archaeology is largely concerned with castles, moated sites, churches, monastic establishments, halls, farm buildings, sites of deserted hamlets and villages, fields, lanes, crosses and wells.

One of the important questions posed to the Survey was: how many of these features have survived in the New Town area, which are at present not recognised, and may be endangered by modern developments?

Let us consider the following brief review.

Castles

The only evidence of a mediaeval castle within the New Town is at Castle Hill, Penwortham.

It was of motte and bailey type and appears to have been at least Saxon in origin, being mentioned in the Domesday Survey of 1086 as belonging to Edward the Confessor. During the reign of Henry III, prior to 1232, a court was held within the castle, but soon after this date it appears that it was allowed to fall into ruin. In 1856 an excavation was carried out, the details of which can be summarised as follows:

'a stone paved building surrounded by timber defences was erected on a low mound at the southern end of the plateau, and it was long inhabited. Earth was found heaped over this habitation to a height of 5 feet and another stone floor laid. The mound was raised again a further 7 feet. No masonry walls were discovered associated with these later phases, and it is not certain which of these phases represent the castle of 1086.'

Subsequent discoveries and discussions have not resolved these problems. The site is undoubtedly an archaeologically important one, capable of producing much more archaeological evidence. The land forms part of the churchyard and some of it has been used as a burial ground in times past, although this use has now stopped. The site is scheduled as an ancient monument.

Moated Homesteads

Moated homestead sites have become recognised in recent years as a widespread feature of later mediaeval times. The moats occur in a variety of shapes, sizes and complexity and are quite distinct from those used for defensive purposes usually associated with castles. The reasons for the construction of these homestead moats are also varied - protection, drainage, water supply, prestige, ornamental and so on. Many of the moats have been filled in and their presence can only be detected from aerial photographs or through fieldwork. The interiors were usually occupied by houses of minor landowners or affluent members of local society. Usually more modern houses and very often farm buildings now occupy the platform site, but where excavation has been possible earlier remains have been discovered providing evidence of this class of society in mediaeval times.

Within the New Town, five moated homestead sites have been established with five other possible ones. Three of the sites, Broughton Tower, Clayton Hall and Lower Farington Hall, either by excavation or visible indications of the moat, are definitely established, and are available for archaeological examination.

Two others, Peacock Hall and Penwortham Hall, are known through documentary evidence and local report; the first is now covered by buildings and a school playing field, the second by houses.

The other five possible moated sites are Lower Burgh Hall, Gillibrand Hall and Astley Hall in Chorley, and Tulketh Hall and Cottam Hall, in north Preston.

Current research reveals that the main period for the construction of these moated sites was late 13th and early 14th century, after which there was a decline until they finally faded out in the 16th century. Dating evidence for the sites within the New Town is slight. A fragment of 14th century pottery was found unstratified at Clayton Hall which comes within the main period. Likewise, documentary reference to the granting of six oaks in 1314 to Gilbert de Singleton, a family later connected with Broughton Tower, may have connections with the building of that moated homestead. There is a further possibility that both these sites may represent new assarts into the forest. Whitaker, writing before 1832 of the Old Priory at Penwortham, describes the building as '...... a humble edifice, three sides of which are entire and inclosed by a moat ......' This reference is interesting from the point of view of date as the moat was presumably constructed when the Priory was converted into a residence by the Fleetwoods around 1543, indicating that moats were still fashionable in the Tudor period.

The three moated sites of Broughton, Clayton-le-Woods, and Farington appear to be of a similar type, covering a rectangular area of around 200 feet square with moat ditches ranging from 20 to 35 feet in width. At Broughton and Clayton-le-Woods the present farm buildings are outside the moat, whilst at Farington they are within it.

In 1977 trial excavations were carried out at Lower Farington. An area in the north-western part of the interior platform was tested by trial trenching which revealed that 19th century buildings had occupied the site. The position of the filled in moat was checked and it was established that the original moat builders had dug right through the band of clay and had penetrated the underlying sand. They then had to reline the moat with clay. No other mediaeval finds or remains were found. A survey of the farmhouse revealed that it had been built between the 17th and 18th centuries and included re-used timbers from a larger and earlier building.

Broughton Tower is perhaps the best preserved of the three sites. The Tower which occupied the interior platform was demolished in 1800 and all that stands there now is a small cottage and a derelict barn. Part of the moat ditch can be quite clearly seen. An informant reported that the Central Electricity Generating Board encountered massive stonework when they were laying cables across the site.

The Hall that occupied the interior platform of the site at Clayton-le-Woods has been vandalised and reduced to a heap of rubble. Fragments of 14th century pottery were recovered from a cutting across the moat ditch a few years ago.

It would be desirable if at least one of these sites could be thoroughly investigated and finally presented, as an ancient monument.

Parish Churches

During this period the main parish churches were established. They have all been enlarged or rebuilt at later stages, although early features can still be seen in some of them. All these buildings and sites are in present use and are not available for archaeological investigation.

Religious Houses

Religious houses are recorded at Penwortham and Preston. Penwortham Priory, attached to the abbey at Evesham, was established in 1087. It was never large, and after the Dissolution the abbey passed into the hands of a local estate, the Fleetwoods, who converted it into a house. The house was rebuilt in the 19th century, but this building has since been demolished and the site is now occupied by housing.

In 1187 a leper hospital was founded in Preston on a site now known as the Maudlands, and was centred around the present site of St Walburge's Church. A chapel associated with this hospital was dedicated in 1293. The hospital fell into disuse sometime after 1399 and the chapel was finally demolished in 1545. Skeletal and coffin remains were encountered during the construction of the railway in the 19th century.

A watching brief and trial trenching was carried out in 1977/78 on the land east of the railway line, known as Maudlands. Whilst a section of the pre-industrial track and a post-mediaeval porringer were discoverd, there were no signs of any features relating to the leper hospital.

However, there is still open land on the other side of the railway cutting, behind St Walburge's Church, which should be archaeologically examined before any future development takes place.

A small Franciscan Friary was founded in 1221 on land which is now occupied by streets and railway sidings just off Marsh Lane. It was described by Leland (c1536) as a 'small square collegiate building with a chapel attached to its quadrangular cloisters'. Despite the present use of the site, there are good chances that archaeological remains survive and given the future co-operation of planning authorities, landowners and British Rail, there is no reason why these should not be recovered.

Documentary evidence indicates that around 1127 the Cistercians had temporary use of buildings or land in Tulketh, although little further detail is known.

Three religious houses appear to have held land within the New Town part of the Leyland Hundred: Penwortham Priory, Cockersand Abbey and the Hospitallers.

Some of the documents record grants in frankalmoign, place names and boundary directions, providing useful clues for landscape studies. The block of land, for example, east of Old Worden in the township of Leyland appears to have been granted by the Clayton family to Cockersand Abbey in the 13th century, and it was then part of the township of Clayton-le-Woods. The granting of land in frankalmoign to religious houses by the lord of the manor was not entirely an act of piety. It was also - in modern terms - a tax dodge, for it freed him of whatever 'knight service' charges that land carried with it. Monastic houses were exempt from 'knight service', so eventually Edward I passed a law curbing this malpractice.

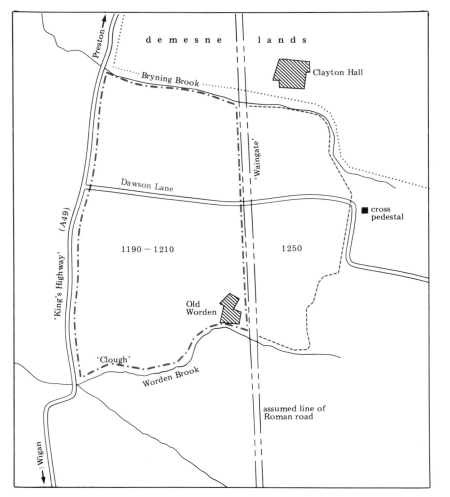

*Probable location of
boundaries of land granted to
Cockersand Abbey*

Key

— ·— *first grant 1190 — 1210*
-------- *second grant 1250*
.... *demesne lands*

↑*north*

Timber Framed Buildings

Halls, farm buildings and cottages represent the most important class of archaeological sites encountered for the post-mediaeval period, and many of them in our area bear witness to their mediaeval origin.

Lancashire shared in common with the rest of the country the use of timber framing and wattle and daub walling for its vernacular buildings. At this time, there was sufficient natural woodland and forest management to supply timber not only for buildings, but for wind and water mills, simple machinery, sluices, bridges, ploughs and waggons. Many grants giving permission for the felling of a limited number of trees have survived in manorial records showing that the use of timber was under strict control. Punishment was meted out to those caught felling trees without permission.

From surviving timber framing, of both box and cruck type, and from foundation plans it is possible to gain some knowledge of the kind of halls, houses, cottages and farm buildings that were in use during mediaeval times.

Some details of mediaeval type buildings have survived in documents. One, dated 1541, describes a hall at Farington, presumably on the moated site of Lower Farington. The following is a brief synopsis:

......the north side of the hall called the ladyehouse, now new built, containing a closet, an entry a ster with a double draught and two new chambers over and under with a double chimney and two galers; the old parlour with the chamber over it on the east part of the great parlour with the draughts thereunto which is now enlarged at the east end and the west end towards the great parlour to the bay windows over and under with the great stair and a new draught with two little closets over and under the south side of the said old parlour with two double chimnies; in one pipe all the waterhowse chamber, the milkhowse under and two chambers over it with two chimnies in one pipe, a closet with a stair to the entry of the said chambers and closet with a draught on the south side of the little yatehouse ......

Further investigations on this site for Leyland Vehicles in 1982 have revealed more details of its history.

Dendrochronological sampling of the re-used timbers from the old farmhouse have shown that some were felled during the 13th century and seem to have been used for a cruck-structured building. Others were felled in the late 15th century, a date which coincides with that of the new building mentioned in the above document.

Lower Farington Hall, Farington
Eastern elevation showing attic window

Lower Farington Hall
Part of upper cruck and door
framing

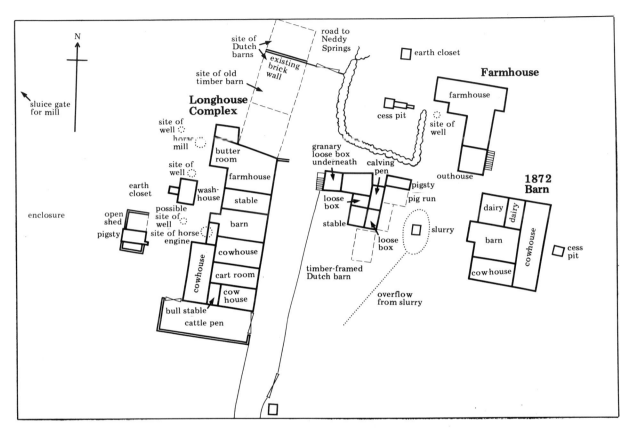

N

sluice gate for mill

site of Dutch barns

road to Neddy Springs

existing brick wall

site of old timber barn

earth closet

Farmhouse

farmhouse

cess pit

site of well

Longhouse Complex

site of well

horse mill

butter room

granary loose box underneath

calving pen

outhouse

1872 Barn

site of well

farmhouse

pigsty

earth closet

wash-house

stable

loose box

pig run

dairy

dairy

possible site of well

barn

stable

cess pit

enclosure

open shed

cowhouse

cowhouse

slurry

barn

pigsty

site of horse engine

cowhouse

loose box

cowhouse

cart room

cow house

timber-framed Dutch barn

overflow from slurry

bull stable

cattle pen

*Lower Farington Hall —
General plan of the farm and
buildings (based on a survey
by Fairhursts, Architects,
1977)*

The majority of 'halls' of the late mediaeval period were not fine Tudor mansions, but the relatively small homes of yeomen. Often, included with the house, under a single roof, was the barn with accommodation for livestock. These buildings were divided into units or 'bays' of approximately 16 feet in length and would vary in size from four to six bays. Humble cottages would consist of one bay only, divided into a bedroom and living room. The barn at Fold's Farm, Ulnes Walton (page 95), appears to have been originally a six bay longhouse, forming part of the hamlet of Folds. The farmhouse at 'My Uncles' Farm in Fulwood (overleaf) in which a pair of cruck blades still remained, was probably of four bay size. Rose Cottage on Runshaw Lane, Euxton was an example of a single bay cottage.

'My Uncles' Farm, Fulwood, Preston

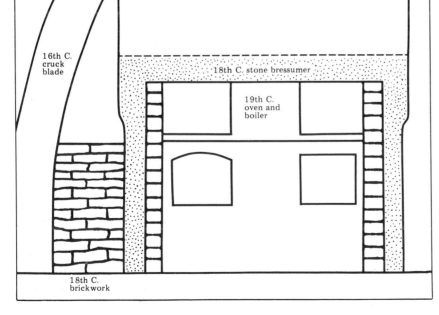

16th C. cruck blade

18th C. stone bressumer

19th C. oven and boiler

18th C. brickwork

Early Brick Buildings

It is an axiom of architectural history that the late 17th century and the 18th century were periods of widespread building. There were several reasons; many timber framed buildings erected during the prosperous Tudor years were in need of repair or renewal, a succession of fires throughout the country, such as the fire of London, created a demand for fireproof materials and there was a growing shortage of timber. Brick became fashionable and in non-stone areas it was the only alternative. In the New Town area stone is very localised, so that widespread use was made of brick. Although much altered, some of these houses still exist, and when their earlier house plans can be identified they will resolve into one, four or six bay units, the number apparently determined by their common land holdings.

Details of the administration and farming methods used for the common fields of mediaeval Lancashire can be gleaned from the manorial court records for areas where these are available. In

Higher Farington Hall, Farington, before demolition, 1977

Measuring and recovering stone slabs from shippon at Higher Farington Hall

the Leyland records there is little mention of the common fields except for fencing, draining, grazing rights, the appointment of moss reeves and so on. Fines are also recorded imposed upon those who transgressed these regulations and for such things as cutting peat, removing sand and digging for clay without permission.

Many earlier buildings were altered or reconstructed using dismantled timbers and replacing wattle and daub exterior walling with loadbearing brick walls. Different types of handmade brick, the larger bricks produced in response to the Brick Tax, mass produced bricks and machine made bricks can be distinguished and are a key factor in dating the construction of buildings and subsequent alterations.

Whilst several halls, farmhouses and barns of the 17th and 18th centuries have survived and their presence noted, only a few have been studied in any detail, either prior to demolition or during alterations. In most cases 19th century extensions or additional farm buildings have obscured the earlier buildings.

Exterior of Tag Farm barn, Ingol, before demolition in 1977
Note Flemish bonding on front elevation

The buildings recorded include:
Higher Farington Hall and farm, Farington
Lower Farington Hall and farm, Farington
Peacock Hall and barn, Dawber's Lane, Euxton
Astley Hall Farmhouse and Gardener's house, Chorley
Bradkirk House, Walton-le-Dale
Tag Farm barn, Ingol
Moss Farm, Longmeanygate, Leyland
My Uncles Farm, Midgery Lane, Fulwood

Many of the former halls of the area which were built by the lesser gentry and prosperous yeomen, such as those at Buckshaw, Worden, Chorley, Woodcock, Clayton, Leyland or Charnock, Crosse, Lower Farington, Broughton Tower and Cottam and others, had, by the end of the 19th century, become farms. Some of these halls have since been demolished, others have become derelict although a few are still in use as farms.

Interior of Tag Farm barn, Ingol

Villages and Hamlets

*Peacock Farm, Euxton —
front and side elevations*

There is very little evidence in the New Town of nucleated villages. The mediaeval townships were composed of a scatter of small hamlets very often bearing the name 'Green' and sometimes centred around a cross. In some cases a small village might have formed the chief place within a township, as in Leyland and Chorley, for example. Some hamlets have survived or have been smothered by later developments; others have disappeared. The settlement of Threlfall in the Haighton area has been a lost hamlet and township since mediaeval times. Cuerden Nook, the chief hamlet of Cuerden, disappeared in the 19th century. There is evidence to suggest that Grimsargh once had a hamlet in the vicinity of the site of the cross near Marsh House Farm. The hamlets and halls that comprised the township of Farington in the 17th century have now almost totally disappeared. What appeared to be its chief hamlet, High Ash, had decayed by the 18th century and the site is now occupied by the head offices of Leyland Vehicles. But not all of the early hamlets have disappeared.

The area around the Seven Stars, Leyland, may be an example of partial survival (page 80). It occupies an important position west of Leyland Church and lies on an ancient route running through the Leyland Hundred from Shevington to Penwortham.

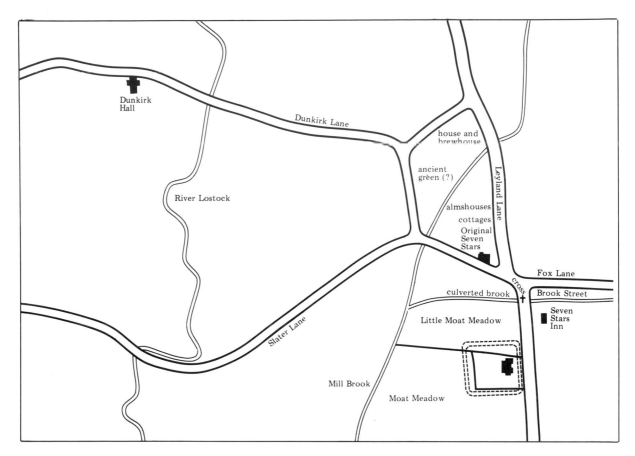

Seven Stars, Leyland

Early map evidence shows that there was a stone cross near the road junction and that a brook, now culverted, ran westwards down Fox Lane.

    The manner in which Dunkirk Lane and Slater Lane join together and finally meet Leyland Lane, forming an enclosed area of land, is suggestive of a former green with Mill Brook flowing southwards across it. Of the scatter of pre-industrial buildings around its edges, only the original Seven Stars Inn, with its 1686 datestone remains. The other building of note in the area is Peacock Hall, an early 17th century brick-built house. In the 19th century the fields behind it were known as 'moat' and 'little moat' meadow, and it has been reported that within living memory there was a 'long hollow in these fields on which you could skate in winter'. Along with other evidence these facts suggest that Peacock Hall was a moated site. It is possible that Seven Stars may have been originally named 'Honkington'. Kuerden, in his 17th century manuscript, mentions this place name as '......a place west of Leyland......'

Crosses

Two other features of mediaeval or earlier origin are crosses and wells. Whilst decorated crosses are amenable to archaeological study, sites of destroyed or removed crosses or cross bases are not quite so informative. However, their presence must be included in an archaeological survey for they can represent early Christian preaching crosses or village, market or boundary crosses.

About 40 have been recorded within the New Town, although only around a quarter of that number have survived. Most of these are just the bases, some of which have had modern shafts inserted or have been converted into war memorials. The only cross to have survived in anything like its original form is the Leyland Village Cross, which stands on its original site in an open space at the corner of Towngate and Church Road, the centre of the original village. It was restored in 1887 when the old well and pump, which accompanied it, were dismantled and replaced by a fountain. Perhaps the most famous cross within the New Town was the High Cross in Preston Market Place. An unsupported tradition records its origin in 1294 and it was at this cross that Henry Beres, Burgess and Recorder of Preston, made his official speech to King James I when he visited the town in 1617. Unfortunately, for the material history of the town, the cross was removed in 1729 for development purposes and although two succeeding obelisks were erected, the last was removed in 1853 and the site is now buried beneath modern development. (Obelisk restored to its original site 1979 for the occasion of

Preston's Octocentenary Year).

It is unlikely that any substantial archaeological evidence still survives that would throw any light on the origin and changing historical significance of the New Town crosses. However, it would be worthwhile examining in more detail, documentary and map evidence for comparison with other regions in the county. Further, the sites of crosses which have not been totally eradicated or buried beneath modern development could be archaeologically examined. Whilst the crosses themselves may have been broken up there could be associated features buried underground which would provide evidence worthy of recovery. Whilst not too much significance must be attributed to these figures it is interesting to note that whilst for most parishes within the New Town one or two crosses are recorded, Preston has seven, Broughton six, Leyland six and Ulnes Walton three.

Wells

About a dozen holy wells, some providing the town water supply, have been recorded within the New Town. All of these are within the Preston area and, although none have survived, the sites of some are known. Some of these wells may date no earlier than the mediaeval period, but there is always the possibility that some of them may be prehistoric in origin and could have been associated with Celtic deities.

It was a common custom in the days of the early Church to Christianise pagan local features, of which wells were one. If any of the recorded well sites are involved in future developments archaeological surveillance would be desirable to check for the presence of Celtic sacrificial objects.

A number of other wells are indicated on ancient maps and in the records. These were dug for the all important water supply, and are often water table wells. The Court Leet Records for Preston for the 17th and 18th centuries contain numerous entries regarding the position of Preston's public draw wells. Perhaps the oldest of these was one at the bottom of Main Sprit Weind.

Apparently, some handsome stonework associated with this well may still survive buried beneath some rather superficial modern development. It should be searched for and recovered if possible at the first opportunity.

The Landscape

Even in these days of urban expansion, fields form the most important part of our local landscapes. Like buildings and documents, they are part of our history; their shapes, dispersion and type of boundaries reveal their age and use. When dated land documents survive they reveal the names of owners, tenants, occasionally details of how the fields were farmed, and, not least in importance, the names that succeeding generations have bestowed upon them.

Place name and field name evidence supported by geographical and palaeo-botanical studies make it clear that the area around the Ribble, in common with much of Lancashire, was at one time well wooded. The word 'Derwent', the original name on the early maps for the River Darwen, for example, means 'the river that flows through the oak woods'.

Generations of settlers from prehistoric times onwards made clearings in the woods and forests. In the early days some of them were only temporary, but later on they became permanent, increasing in size to include open fields for crops, pastures and cattle corrals. The adjacent woodland was used for pannage, timber for buildings and the collecting of firewood. Where extensive peat mosses occurred, such as those near Leyland, they too were used for grazing in the summer and the peat for fuel in the winter.

Place name evidence indicated that there were a number of Celtic settlements scattered throughout the New Town in late prehistoric, Roman and early Dark Age times.

When the Anglo-Saxon invaders entered the area they reorganised the administration of the land, taking over some of the indigenous Celtic settlements, and opened up new land for expansion.

Of the hundreds that made up the Palatine of Lancashire, the New Town is involved in three; the main one being Leylandshire, the other two meeting in the Preston area are Amounderness and Blackburnshire. These Hundreds may well have represented tribal areas in Celtic times, as suggested by place names containing the element 'eccles'. Whilst not a common element it occurs five times in Lancashire, in five of the six Hundreds, for example, there is Eccleston' in Leylandshire, 'Great and Little Eccleston' in Amounderness, and 'Eccleshill' in Blackburnshire.

As we have seen, the Vikings, apart from raiding and destroying settlements in their longships, which could have penetrated far up the Ribble and some way up the River Darwen, also opened up new land for settlements along the Lancashire coast and around the Ribble. But it was the Normans, who were descendants of Vikings from the north of France, that established the character of England's mediaeval land administration and Lancashire was no exception.

The mediaeval manor with its church, village, manor house and common fields was not, however, typical of Lancashire.

The topography, broken up by marshlands, narrow valleys and moorlands, and the climate with a tendency to high rainfalls and late spring frosts made it unsuitable for large scale arable agriculture. Lancashire has, up to recent years, been mainly a livestock and dairy farming county. Thus it was that many of the earlier Celtic traditions of scattered hamlets with small, individually held enclosures, as well as common fields, survived in many areas throughout the Middle Ages. In all probability they represented the best method of farming the land.

The system of landholding, known as severalty, was also of Celtic origin. It was a system in which the land was divided between the heirs. The dividing of a holding and its rights between several children of succeeding generations would result in considerable fragmentation and a point would be reached when the holdings were too small to be workable. Thus it was, out of necessity, that the family had often to work together as a group. Consequently, this system induced much selling, buying and transferring of land and also the enclosure of new land or assarting from waste and common holdings.

The following examples refer to Farington:

'......an assart in Bernardescocs-hutte .... ascending Town Brook to the ditch between land of Ugthred and land of late Welsh John, ascending the ditch to the end of Farington ......'
possibly 13th century

'Robert Yatton prior of Penwortham to Henry, son of Sir William Farington, Anne his wife and William his eldest son - a cottage and 1½ acres (approximately 3 statutory acres) of land late enclosed by Sir William Farington on the common pasture of Farington......'
a lease dated 7th December 1502

Rights on common land and the size of a freeman's, or charterer's dwelling, as well as cottager's, were determined by the size of their landholdings. The Farington Estate map of 1725 shows, for example, the remains of the strip holdings in Leyland's town fields and it is quite clear that these were held by several people who farmed them along with the enclosed fields adjacent to their house or farm.

One aspect of the local mediaeval landholding system was that it undoubtedly set the stage for farming developments in the later 18th and 19th centuries by giving the individual farmer a degree of independence. Obviously limited by his available capital, size of labour force and conditions of his lease, he could make his own decisions on how he farmed the land of his enclosed fields. His counterpart in the Midlands, for example, had to abide by decisions made in the manorial court based on the agreement of all the villagers whose land was scattered strip holdings in the common fields.

The piecemeal enclosure of land that had been continuing from time immemorial increased during the 18th century, and particularly towards its end, when improving landlords, inspired by the new agricultural methods, were putting considerable capital into land.

Ambrye Meadows, Leyland

Two interesting plans (below) illustrate the final stages of
the common field system and its ultimate enclosure at the end of
the 18th century. The indenture accompanying the enclosure plan
makes it quite clear that the purpose of the enclosure is to make
the fields ......'more fitting for the new agricultural methods'.

The two plans are concerned with an area of about 12 acres
of water meadows known as Ambrye Meadows, situated in the south-
west corner of the township of Leyland. Place name and
geographical evidence indicate that these meadows formed part of
an early Celtic settlement and that in mediaeval times they were
common fields in which the inhabitants of Leyland had holdings.

Ambrye Meadows —
left, pre-enclosure 1737
right, enclosure 1785
(based on Robert Welch's
Estate Plan 1737)

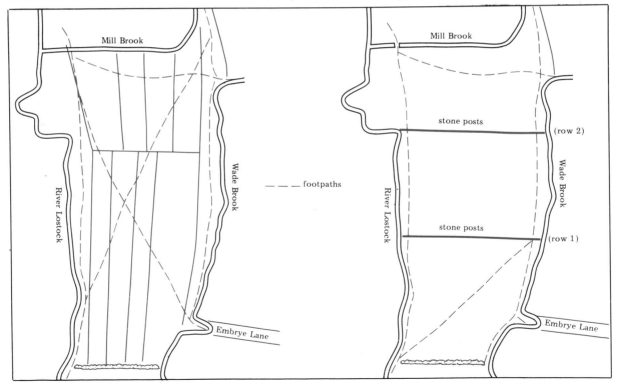

Ambrye Meadows — stone posts

A plan of the common field landholdings is included in an inventory to the will of Robert Welch, yeoman and is dated 1737. Details of the strips are shown, and also the names of those who held them, and it showed that some strips had been enclosed and were permanent whilst others were moveable. The second document refers to the enclosure of these meadows in 1785. It is an enclosure by the common consent of all those who had holdings. The meadows were now to be divided into three parts marked by two lines of stone posts with through rails (above). Many of these stones still survive and one line of them has been restored as a feature of Leyland's local history.

The Nineteenth Century
& Industrial Archaeology

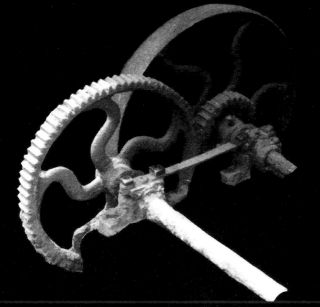

Agriculture

The history of 18th and 19th century agriculture emerged during the Survey as a feature of importance on two counts. Firstly, in its own right as an aspect of Lancashire's industrial history, and secondly, as the starting place for archaeological landscape investigation. The latter has, of necessity, to adopt the retrogressive approach to history which commences with the present day situation and works patiently backwards in time until the evidence runs out. This was one of the methods employed in the Survey.

The agricultural history of these two centuries was also seen to be a much neglected part of Lancashire's history, although there is abundant evidence in the form of farm buildings, fields and documentary sources, including Tithe Award plans and early editions of the Ordnance Survey maps.

It is sufficient to say for our present purposes that as the Industrial Revolution progressed not only were existing towns and villages enlarged but new ones were built. As we shall see (page 101) Preston built itself a 'new town' in the Moor Brook area and Nelson, in East Lancashire, did not exist when the first Ordnance Survey map was published around 1838. Thus was the rural landscape affected, but it was also affected by increased agricultural activities. The taking in of new land by clearing and draining, the extensive use of marling in parts of West Lancashire and the Fylde, more intensive use for dairy farming and the creation of new farms were amongst the most important of the new developments.

The response of agriculture to the new and rapidly expanding local markets and the way in which it took advantage of every development in transport, machinery and new sources of power, in addition to purely agricultural developments, was an important aspect of Lancashire's industrial greatness - an aspect which has not been sufficiently recognised.

Investigations into the farms that came within the Survey's purview revealed examples of the type of farm buildings that were in current use before extensive commercial farming developed and before the day of the small farmers and cottagers, who combined farming with some craft or trade, was over. It was seen that many of the small farms had expanded, taking in more land; new houses were built or old ones repaired and enlarged and new and improved types of farm buildings were added.

Moss Farm, Longmeanygate, Leyland

Moss Farm, Longmeanygate, can be taken as an example.

In its later days this farm appeared to comprise mainly 19th century buildings of little historical merit.

However, documentary evidence and a close examination of the building fabric and the shape of the longhouse type of farmhouse and barn proved it to be otherwise. 17th century survey records showed that it had been part of the Farington Estate for over 300 years. In these early times it was known as 'Wilson's' with two small buildings, a house and a barn, and farmed about 13 statutory acres. A plan of 1725 showed that the two buildings occupied the site of the later farmhouse and barn. Examination of the existing structure, aided by 19th century map evidence, made it clear that at some time in the early 19th century the two buildings had been partly demolished and then rebuilt under a common roof, resulting in a larger house and a larger barn (page 92). In the latter part of the 18th century the land holdings had been increased to 33 statutory acres, and then in the early 19th century to over 50 acres (see page 93). The new land was mostly reclaimed moss land that had been enclosed on Leyland Moss after peat cutting had left it waste. Wilson's, now known as Moss House, was one of the larger holdings on the Farington Estate at this time - 1838.

In the latter half of the 19th century, a new range of farm buildings was erected to the south of the original longhouse. A stock yard was formed with a large, new Dutch barn adjacent. There were also alterations to the house and the barn which included attic accommodation for labourers living in. The farm was now known as 'Moss Farm'.

The end of the 19th century saw further developments. A small building was erected close to the farmhouse for the purpose

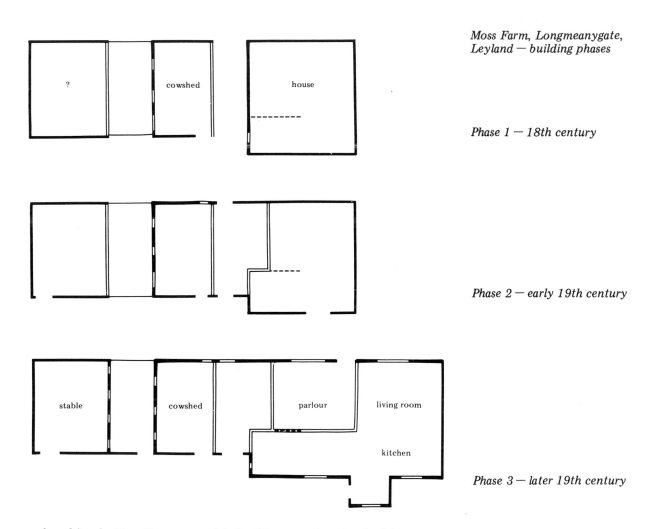

Phase 1 — 18th century

?   cowshed   house

Phase 2 — early 19th century

Phase 3 — later 19th century

stable   cowshed   parlour   living room   kitchen

of making butter. It was provided with a small water turbine which drew on the local water supply, and its purpose was to drive the churns. Also dateable to this period was a small horse engine, or 'horse-gin' (page 94) which had survived the past seventy years and was, happily, recovered before demolition. This gin had been used seemingly for grinding cattle food and was

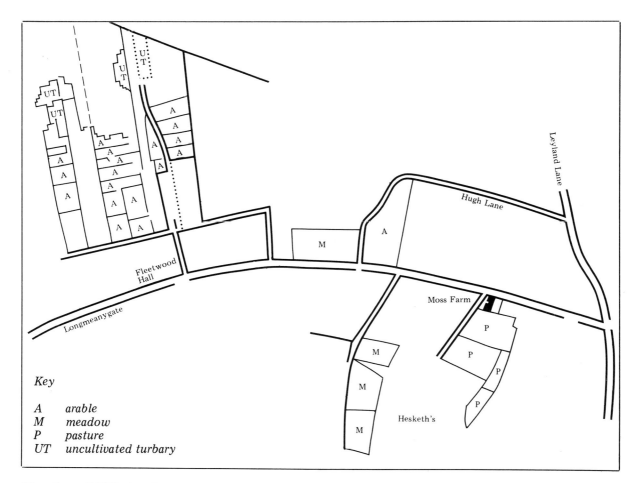

Key

A	arable
M	meadow
P	pasture
UT	uncultivated turbary

Moss Farm (1838) showing
land holdings

	A	R	P
Land around farm	6	2	2
Land down lane	5	3	2
Land on Longmeanygate	8	2	21
Land on moss	29	3	20
	50	3	15

Arable	—	20 acres approx.
Meadow	—	14 acres approx.
Pasture	—	6½ acres approx.
Uncultivated turbary	—	10½ acres approx.

obviously, along with the water turbine, part of the equipment for more intensive dairy farming and butter production. Horse-gins were common on the local farms during the 18th and 19th centuries. They were of various sizes and were adapted to do various jobs such as threshing, churning butter, chopping straw and cattle food, and even washing clothes. One was recorded at Lower Farington Hall where it was used for pumping slurry from a farmyard tank.

'Horse gin' at Moss Farm, Longmeanygate, Leyland

Folds, Ulnes Walton

In 1980 the structure of the derelict barn at Folds became unsafe through persistent vandalism. It was decided that the remains should be dismantled so that the surviving timbers could be recovered and any architectural details of interest recorded.

Three pairs of cruck trusses and their associated timbers were donated to South Ribble Borough Council for re-erection at Worden Hall in Leyland.

With the assistance of the Archaeology Group of Wellfield High School, Leyland, excavations of the site were carried out in the Augusts of 1980, 1981 and 1982. Three sites were examined: the barn, the house and a test trench, which revealed two early field drains.

In 1980, the accumulated debris from the floor of the barn was cleared, revealing a mid 19th century shippon floor, with the remains of an earlier 17th century floor lying beneath. A number of alteration

Folds Farm barn, Ulnes Walton, showing exposed cruck truss, 1976

phases were detected and there had been, at all periods, extensive re-use of original building materials.

In 1981, the outside of the foundations on the northern side of the barn, a quantity of building and demolition debris - strips of lead from diamond paned windows, sawn-off wooden pegs, fragments of handmade brick and post-mediaeval pottery - were found buried beneath a 19th century cinder track. These finds suggest that in the late 17th or early 18th century an existing building was dismantled and a new one built in which handmade bricks had been used for the first time. Stone plinths and much of the timber cruck-framing from the earlier building were re-used.

Some sixty yards to the east of the barn, the buried foundations of a house were revealed. The excavated features included the stone flagged floor at the kitchen end and a doorway leading into a cobbled backyard. Edging this yard was a seven foot lintel from a stone fireplace and a water trough. The purpose of these stone objects in this position is not clear. However, the handmade brick, the post-mediaeval pottery and re-used stone suggested that this building was contemporary with the rebuilding of the barn.

A trial trench, some 100 yards to the east of the house revealed two drains, almost side by side, of the early soakaway type. The first drain was nearly three feet deep and was simply a dug trench penetrating the underlying boulder clay and back filled with soil and fragments of burnt stone from a kiln or a furnace and sherds of pottery. The latter was of the green and brown lead-glazed earthenware type; some of the pieces rejoined and others were decorated with a thumb impressed pattern. They had, originally, been part of large storage jars of the type in common use during the 14th century.

The second drain was about a foot to eighteen inches below the top soil and was carefully made with fragments of handmade brick, brick wasters, cobbles and sherds of post-mediaeval pottery.

In 1982 further investigation of these drains was carried out as a training excavation, involving pupils from Wellfield School, Leyland, and Tulketh High School, Preston.

More pottery sherds were discovered, some of which

conjoined with fragments found earlier. The drains, or ditches, were seen to be more complex and had been re-dug more than once. The site awaits continued excavation.

Documentary and field research revealed the presence of a dovecote and a dole lane leading to the mediaeval water meadows down by the River Lostock.

The archaeological work has made it clear that beneath this ordinary looking field there lies a lot of buried history and an archaeological site of importance.

Cheese Making

It was not only the larger farms such as Moss Farm, Higher Farington and Lower Farington for example, that were successful. In the first half of the 19th century a farmer and his family who were farming Butler's Farm in Leyland Lane, Leyland, were producing during the summer months around 100 cheeses of 30lbs each in weight. They achieved this output from 27 acres supporting six milk cows and a few followers. They also won prizes for their cheeses three years in succession at the County Agricultural Show. Cheese making was a speciality in the Leyland and Preston area, as witnessed by the numerous examples of stone cheese presses found lying about farmyards and sometimes built into later farm buildings.

Preston

It would be wrong to finish this chapter without mentioning the semi-rural character of towns like Preston. A glance at the 1838 Tithe Award Plan for Preston shows, even at that date, how many fields there were in and around Preston. A newspaper report in the 1830s graphically describes how the apprentice of a chandler situated in Tithebarn Street was knocked down at 8 o'clock in the morning by a fast stage-coach whilst driving his master's cows.

Communal Bake-houses

Evidence of the transition from rural life to industrial during the 19th century was revealed during a watching brief on a building site at the Maudlands, Preston. The area was previously occupied by streets of operatives' houses built during the middle of the 19th century. During the redevelopment when trenches

Remains of communal bakehouse with two ovens, Maudlands, Preston

were being dug a brick feature was encountered below the surface. It proved, on archaeological examination, to be a pair of baker's ovens built below ground in an outside cellar in what had been the backyard of an end terraced house.

The ovens themselves, one of them 10 feet long, actually extended beneath the backyards of the neighbouring houses. The entire complex had been cunningly planned into the standard street development. It had obviously been a communal bakehouse which could be used by the women of the neighbouring streets for baking their bread and cooking their hot pots. The cellar had been filled in to make an open backyard many years ago, and no-one knew there had been a bake-house there.

During the investigation two adjacent wells were discovered nearby in what had been the backyard of another house, where they had probably provided water for a wash-house or for brewing beer. A local person who knew the locality as a child, just before the turn of the century, reported that six cows were kept by a cow keeper behind one of the terraced houses in a small shippon which occupied the backyard. The cows were let out in the summer and were allowed to graze on nearby banks of the Lancaster Canal. Watchful mothers kept their children indoors whilst the cows frisked about in the street after their winter confinement.

It is interesting to note that there was no obvious documentary evidence of these early industrial housing features, and that their recognition has been the result of archaeological excavation and enquiries, following the reported discovery by the contractors.

The communal bake-house in Brackenbury Street, Preston is discussed on page 104.

Industrial Archaeology

Within the county during the past few years there has been increasing interest and developments in industrial archaeology.

It seems at long last, that Lancashire is awakening to the fact that it has a rich industrial heritage.

The opening of the British Commercial Vehicle Museum at Leyland has been a landmark and the publication of books on handloom weavers cottages[1], the cotton mills of Preston[2], and the Victorian domestic architecture of Preston[3] and school study packs, reflect a rapidly growing interest amongst schools and colleges.

However, it must be remembered that industrial archaeology is a comparatively new branch of archaeology which has not yet fully established itself. In general terms it sees itself recording, studying and selectively conserving various manifestations of the industrial landscape before they are swept away by the rapid changes that are taking place in technology and building redevelopment. Demolition is widespread, and in this demolition the industrial archaeologist can find opportunity for examining buildings and searching for evidence of early phases which have been masked by subsequent developments. The accumulative evidence from such surveys is providing a body of data of all kinds; information which cannot be obtained from any other source. Many of these changes, important to the historian, were not recorded at the time they happened. Many industrial records have been destroyed as firms have gone out of business or have been absorbed into larger concerns.

Therefore the importance of continued recording and investigation of standing buildings and other industrial features, cannot be over emphasised.

1 *J G Timmins, 1977, University of Lancaster*
  'Handloom Weavers Cottages in Central Lancashire'
2 *T C Dickinson, 1981, Preston Curriculum Development Centre*
  'Industrial Archaeology of the Preston Cotton Industry'
3 *Nigel Morgan, 1982, Preston Curriculum Development Centre*
  'Victorian Housing in Preston'

Preston

Preston seems to have been generally later than other neighbouring industrial towns in developing its textile and related industries. Unlike them, it had no readily available natural resources in the form of coal, building stone, etc. which all had to be brought by transport from other parts of the county. Its position on the Ribble restricted its use of canals so that it was not until the railway networks were established in the 1840s that Preston's major industrial developments took place.

In Preston, twenty-eight sites were visited, cursorily examined and photographed. Of these twenty-four were mills, three were railway stations and one was the Corn Exchange. The mills mostly date from the middle of the 19th century to the early years of the present one. The majority are fulfilling secondary purposes and are in good condition, although modernisation has resulted in the demolition of earlier features such as stoke houses, chimneys and minor buildings. Of two mill complexes, or early industrial estates, one, Shelley Road Mills, was found to be derelict with demolition taking place.

Documentary research and fieldwork carried out in tracing the history of the 19th century culverting of Moor Brook threw interesting light on the early industrial development of Preston.

In the early 19th century the land forming the Moor Brook valley, extending from Preston Moor in the east to Preston Marsh and the Ribble in the west, was predominantly a rural area of small fields and market gardens. In the 18th century it was crossed only by the stage-coach road to Lancaster, then followed the canal and in the 19th century the two railways. Its industrial development was inevitable.

It appears that as early as 1817 Preston Corporation were collaborating with local landowners and evolving schemes for new housing and urban development of these rural areas, including the common land on Preston Moor.

The Greenbank Estate forms an interesting example. It will be seen from the 1813 plan (page 102) that the Andertons owned the estate and that in 1817 (page 103) they were offering it for

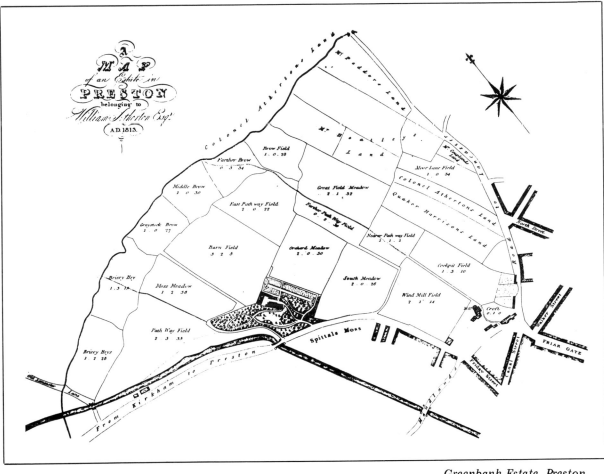

Greenbank Estate, Preston, 1813

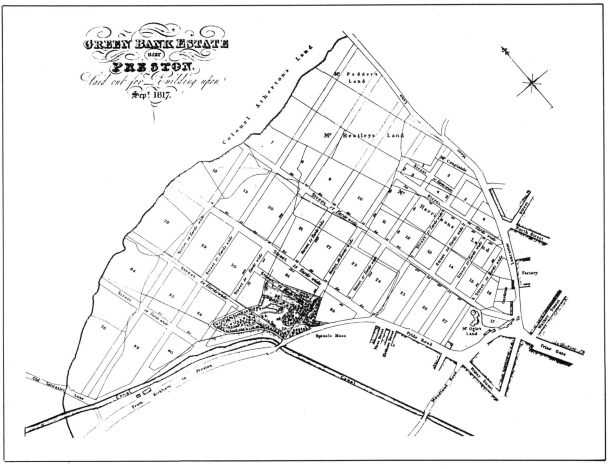

Greenbank Estate, Preston,
1817

sale with outline street planning. This estate was bought by Thomas Tomlinson, a London barrister of local origin, and his brother. The 1838 Tithe Award Plan shows that they had let off some of the land to tenant farmers and the remainder they had retained for sand quarrying and brick making. They had also begun the process of culverting the Moor Brook and filling in its valley to a depth of 30 feet in some places. During the following decades this reclaimed land was built over, piecemeal, by speculative builders who had to adhere to the street plan and various building regulations. When the new houses were built they were put up for auction, bought, and then rented to millworkers.

Brackenbury Street, Preston: corner shop, dwellinghouse and three other houses

Note: the door, centre, opens onto steps which lead down into the cellar bake-house. A blocked-up door, immediately to its left gave access to the living room of the house.

An interesting example of this process, and one which links up with our discoveries at the Maudlands, can be seen at Brackenbury Street in the Gallows Hill district. The land was formerly part of the common land of Preston Moor and was owned by Preston Corporation. They sold it to Thomas Tomlinson, the same as mentioned above, and he leased it to a Henry Porter, bricksetter, who built on it a corner shop, with dwelling-house and bake-house, and three adjoining houses, sometime in 1860 (opposite). The shop became the local grocer's and the bake-house was a communal bake-house, the trade for which was conducted from the dwelling-house at the back. One pound loaf tins were loaned to the housewives who brought their bread to be baked. In 1979 this cellar bake-house was discovered, reasonably intact, after being closed up for over sixty years. There was one large oven, over 14 feet long, and within it were the remains of a hundred or so rusty baking tins, two peels and two charcoal trays. The oven had been heated by coke originally, but later the firebox was blocked up and the oven heated by charcoal.

It is becoming obvious that archaeology and building investigations have a part to play in rediscovering the social and industrial history of 19th century Preston.

Lancaster Canal Tramway

The remains of the Lancaster Canal Tramway, from the canal basin in Corporation Street, Preston to Walton Summit, were investigated during the Survey. This tramway which operated for about 50 years, opening in 1802, linked the two canal basins of Preston and Walton Summit, which were separated by the Ribble. The Walton Summit basin was filled in when the M61 Motorway was built a few years ago. The waggons on this tramway were drawn by horses, assisted by stationary steam engines at the steep inclines at Avenham and the Summit. It was one of the earliest tramways of its kind in the country and became obsolete when the canal system was superceded by the railways in the middle of the 19th century. This tramway seems to be the only industrial monument that evokes any local interest.

At Stocksbar Cottage, near Summit Farm, a small stone single-storey building still stands, which, according to early map evidence, was connected with the weighing machine (page 106). Beyond this point there is a double track up to the Summit where

the waggons were hauled up by steam.

Beyond Summit Farm, a stretch of sleeper stones was exposed and incorporated in the new road landscaping. Other sleeper stones, disturbed by development, were recovered and stored. It was felt at the time that this exposed stretch of sleeper stones was not the original trackway, the sleeper stones being laid close together when they should have been 3 feet apart (opposite).

In 1977 a trial excavation was carried out along the verge of the hedge opposite the small stone building at Stocksbar Cottage.

This page and opposite: the Lancaster Canal Tramway at Walton Summit Employment Area near Bamber Bridge

Top, a small building associated with weighing machine

Above left, re-used sleeper stones for farm track above Summit Farm and right, the line of tramway near Gough Lane, Walton Summit

The purpose was to test whether or not any evidence might have survived which should throw light on the construction of the weighing machine or any other equipment at this important point along the tramway. No features of this type were encountered, owing to the limited area of ground available for excavation. However, part of the trackway was discovered, lying in situ, beneath a further stretch of re-used sleeper stones identically laid to those beyond Summit Farm.

It seems that after the tramway was abandoned and finally dismantled in 1868 the farmer of Summit Farm built himself a farm road from these sleeper stones which not only went towards the Summit, but for some way in the opposite direction, probably linking the farm with Gough Lane.

The use of a metal detector revealed buried rails between the tramway hedgerows beyond Gough Lane. There is scope for more fieldwork and excavation concerning the tramway in this area when opportunity permits and when ideas are clearer on how the vestiges of this historic tramway can be most appropriately enshrined in the landscape and presented as an historic monument.

Leyland, South Ribble and Chorley

Linen Weavers

During a survey of the township of Clayton-le-Woods, evidence of flax and hemp growing and linen weaving was revealed, from the early 16th century onwards. Post mortem inventories of the 16th and 17th centuries, of both men and women living in this area, gave details. Flax and tow, linen yarn, pairs of looms and other equipment was mentioned. It seems that some of the flax growers were also money-lenders.

The handloom weavers' cottages with ground floor loom shops, and perhaps some with cellars, were originally used for linen weaving. Cotton and linen weaving are very similar in many ways, and it seems likely that in the late 18th and 19th century cotton handloom weaving was founded on the earlier linen industry.

Field names gave some indication of flax growing. In Clayton-le-Woods, for example, a small field behind a handloom weavers' cottage in Sheep Hill Lane had the name 'Higher Yarn Croft' in 1838.

Early Textiles

From the late 18th century to some time after 1851, cottage

handloom weaving of cotton flourished and declined.

In Chorley, Leyland, Clayton-le-Woods, and Cuerden, rows of terraced handloom weavers' cottages with cellar loomshops were built. Many have survived to the present day, and can be easily recognised by the steps leading to the front door. The best known examples are in Fox Lane, Leyland.

The Census Returns for Clayton Town for 1851 show that handloom weaving was still being carried out by the husband, wife or sons living in the handloom weavers' cottages.

From the evidence of a letter written in 1784 and an estate plan, it appears that calico bleaching was being carried out at Dovecote in Clayton-le-Woods. The pond and leets still survive on this site.

Birkacre, Chorley

At Birkacre in Chorley, 18th century estate maps and documentary evidence have revealed interesting developments from the mediaeval corn mill and fish ponds to early iron smelting, and the replacing of the corn mill by a water powered spinning mill — leased to Richard Arkwright in 1777, and destroyed by riots in 1779. It eventually became a bleach works which survived until recent years.

Later, in the 19th century, coal mining was developed and a mineral line constructed from Birkacre to a coal depot on Strand Road.

Lower Kem Mill, Clayton-le-Woods

The remains of an early bleach and print works have been located on the River Lostock at the southern end of the Cuerden Valley Park.

Documentary evidence revealed its origins prior to 1838, when it was powered by a water wheel. It ceased to exist in 1914 when it was burnt down. The site was used as a sheep farm until

Map of Cuerden and Clayton-le-Woods (right)

Halls

1 Lostock Hall	A1
2 Woodcock Hall	(s)A1
3 Cuerden Hall	A2
4 Clayton Hall	(s)A3
5 Crook Hall	B3
6 New Crook Hall	(s)B3

Farms

7 Hawksclough	B1
8 Clock House	A2
9 Cuerden's	A2
10 Woodcocks	A2
11 Dovecote	B2
12 Little Dovecote	(s)B2
13 Calderbanks	B2
14 Fowlers	B2
15 Abbots	B2
16 Town End	A2
17 Lancaster House	(s)A3
18 Martindales	(s)B2
19 Higher Woodend	(s)B2
20 Lower Woodend	B2
21 Carvers	B2
22 Heald House	A3

Inns

23 Parkers Arms	(s)A1
24 George and Dragon	(s)B2
25 Pear Tree (coaching inn)	(s)B2
26 Halfway House	B2
27 Toll House	B2
28 Dandy Bridge	A1
29 Cuerden Pinfold	(s)A1
30 Clayton Pinfold	(s)B2

Schools

31 Cuerden School	(s)A1
32 Clayton School	(s)B2

Mills

33 Corn Mill	(s)A1
34 Lostock Mill	A1
35 Corn Mill and Leet	(s)B2
36 Kem Mill	(s)B3
37 Handloom weavers cottages	B2
40 18th century bleaching bleaching	(s)B2
41 Lostock Fold	A1
42 Tunnel	A2
43 Roman Catholic chapel	(s)B1
44 Ice house	B2
44a Reservoir & hydraulic rams	B2

Hamlets

45 Cuerden Nook	(s)A1
46 Cuerden Green	(s)A1
47 Old Cuerden	(s)A1
48 Bottoms	(s)A2
49 Lydiate	A2
50 Clayton Green	B2
51 Clayton Town	B2
52 Moss Houses	(s)A2

Possible Prehistoric and Roman

53 Hawksclough settlement	B2
54 Dovecote settlement	B2
55 Roman road	A2
56 Roman hole	B2
57 Early fields	B2

Possible Dark Age and Mediaeval

58 Rangletts	B2

59 Castle (shooting lodge)	A1
60 Faldworthings (sheep)	A1
61 Town fields	A1
62 Smithy	A1
63 Stoney Lane	A1
64 Early fields	A1
65 Water meadows	B2
66 Cross Base	(s)A1
67 Cross Base	(s)B1
68 Cross Base	(s)B2

(s) — site of

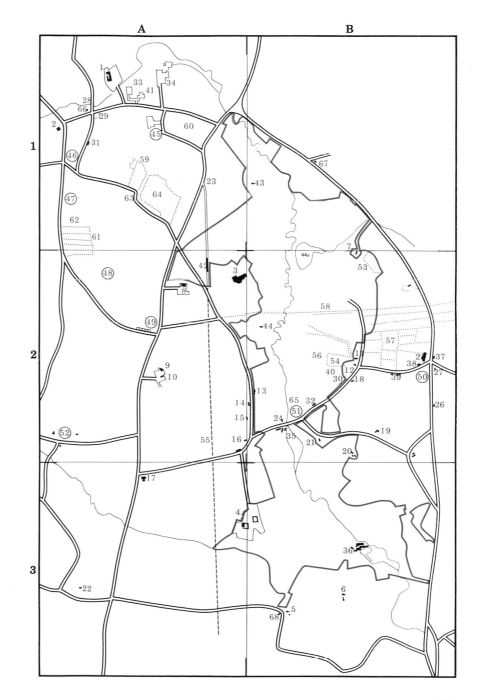

111

Glossary

agger	a slightly raised bank on which the Roman engineers built stretches of road
assarts	pieces of land brought into cultivation from the natural woodlands
cruck-truss	a timber frame shaped like a letter 'A'
dendrochronology	a method of dating using tree-ring growth
frankalmoign	a land gift exempt from military obligation
marling	fertilising land with lime-rich clay dug from beneath, hence marlpits
moss reeve	officer in charge of mosslands
palaeo-botanical	the study of botanical remains in ancient soils and peat
pannage	pasture for pigs in woodland
peels	a flat sheet of metal attached to a long handle for conveying loaf tins in and out of large baking ovens
podsol	bleached sand soil, poor in humus
porringer	a small basin-like vessel from which soup or porridge could be eaten

Index of Place Names